OUTLINE PLAN
- OF -
MIDDLESEX CO.
CONN.
Scale 2¼ Miles to the inch

Meridian

*This beautiful, illustrated book
was made possible thanks to
the generous support of the
following sponsors:*

**The Connecticut Light
and Power Company**

Farmers & Mechanics Bank

Bernie Fields Jewelers

Liberty Bank

Middlesex Hospital

**Middlesex Mutual
Assurance Company**

Wesleyan University

———————————

*An in-kind donation
was provided by:*

**Pratt & Whitney
A United Technologies Company**

Long Ago, Not Far Away

An Illustrated History of Six Middlesex County Towns

Edited by
Julia Perkins, Bernadette S. Prue and Claudette Kosinski
for The Greater Middletown Preservation Trust

We would like to thank
the following businesses for their
support of this project:

Gold Circle
Connecticut Yankee
Atomic Power Company

Covenant Village of Cromwell
and Pilgrim Manor

Silver Circle
Bidwell Industrial Group Inc.

The Hartford Courant

Labco Welding Inc.

The Lyman Farm Inc.

The Middlesex Supply Company

Peter B. Nelson, DDS P.C.

Rice, Davis, Daley & Krenz, Inc.

Simply Elegant

Copyright © by The Greater Middletown
Preservation Trust

All rights reserved, including the right to reproduce
this work in any form whatsoever without permission
in writing from the publisher, except for brief
passages in connection with a review.

The Donning Company/Publishers
184 Business Park Drive, Suite 106
Virginia Beach, Virginia 23462

Steve Mull, General Manager
Debra Y. Quesnel, Project Director
Tracey Emmons-Schneider, Director of Research
Dawn Kofroth, Production Manager

Library of Congress Cataloging-in-Publication Data

Long ago, not far away : an illustrated history of six
Middlesex County towns / by the Greater
Middletown Preservation Trust.
        p.   cm.
Includes bibliographical references (p.   ) and
index.
      ISBN 0-89865-976-0 (alk. paper)
      1. Cities and towns—Connecticut—Middlesex
County—History—Pictorial works. 2. Middlesex
County (Conn.)—History. Local. I. Greater
Middletown Preservation Trust (Middletown,
Conn.)
F102.M6L66 1996
974.6'009732—dc20   96-30300
                                                      CIP

Dedication

We dedicate this book to Ann Street.
Her commitment to historic preservation
has inspired many throughout Middlesex
County to seek to understand how the patterns
of the past invest today's decisions with the
power to affect the future of our communities.

Contents

Foreword

As I gaze out at Lake Pocotopaug from my home in East Hampton on this first day of spring, 1996, I think back to the 1650s when this area of Connecticut was being settled. Native Americans populated the land first and had their own culture, and the towns, roads, bridges, and buildings that we take for granted today obviously didn't exist. To appreciate our proud history you have to go back to those early days, when the farmer had to clear his fields of stones as he struggled to earn a meager living from the soil; or back to the shipbuilding that took place in each river town; or to the industries that grew up along the streams and rivers in all our towns; and finally on to the present day when many of our communities are bedroom towns as we commute to distant places for employment.

If you're curious about how East Hampton, Cromwell, Portland, Middlefield, Durham, or Haddam were first settled, then you'll thoroughly enjoy reading this book. It's a fascinating history, accompanied by priceless photographs. Although these six towns have changed greatly and have individual personalities, they are similar in many ways: all have historic buildings, village greens, church steeples, winding country roads, stone walls, old abandoned foundations, lakes, brooks, streams, rivers, forests, and fields.

In these busy and complicated days, take time to appreciate how fortunate we are to have these ancient surroundings, yet live in the present and be able to look forward to the future.

After reading these town histories, do as I have done many times: take a leisurely ride, stop, and explore these six communities to get the true feeling and flavor of our heritage. I hope you will agree that we must do our utmost to preserve and protect this wonderful place.

BILL O'NEILL
Governor of Connecticut
1980–1991

Acknowledgments

Many, many months of effort have gone into the publication of *Long Ago, Not Far Away.*

That this effort was expended by a cadre of volunteers makes this volume truly remarkable. This cast of thousands spent hour after hour collecting pictures, writing and editing text, writing captions, developing a marketing plan and materials, and all the rest of the myriad of tasks that resulted in this treasure.

We would like to thank Bernadette S. Prue, the indefatigable chair of our committee, whose vision for *Long Ago, Not Far Away* has made the book what it is. We are grateful for the talents of Julie Perkins, whose editorial skills transformed a million disparate pieces into *Long Ago, Not Far Away.* We thank Claudette Kosinski for traveling near and far to collect pictures from historical societies and private collections, and for the enthusiasm she brought to the entire project and Dan Davis, for his hard work in editing the picture captions. Thank you to Helene Loveless for bringing Cromwell's history up to date, as well as for writing Cromwell's picture captions. We thank the following diligent and talented volunteers who wrote captions, edited text, collected photographs, and worked on the marketing campaign: Chris Brunson, Bill Earls, Darren Fava, Peter Frenzel, Lisa Goldreich, Laurel Goodgion, Amy Harkenreader, Jane Harris, Kathy O'Connell, Sarah O'Connor, Lynn Parrott, Bernard Prue, Steve Rocco, Elise Roenigk, Bill Stowe, Barbara Warner and Sandy Weiman. We would also like to thank the families of our volunteers for their patience while their loved ones worked long hours on this undertaking.

We thank Lois Donohue, Fran Korn, Nancy Eklund, Savitri Szufnarowski, Lynette Brayshaw, Doris Sherrow, Gail Porteus, J. Paul Loether, Anna Mae

Spooner, Jan Sweet, and Dione Longley of the local historical societies for their support of this project by providing us with fascinating information and generous access to their wonderful collections and editorial assistance. Special thanks go to the individuals who responded to our request for pictures with the cherished photos you will find throughout *Long Ago, Not Far Away.*

Former Governor William O'Neill wrote the Foreword which reveals his enthusiasm for the book and his love for the area. Diana McCain of the Connecticut Historical Society wrote the Introduction, which brilliantly puts the history of this area into larger context. Matt Polansky brought energy, skill, and efficiency to reproducing hundreds of photographs. To these three we extend our appreciation as well as to Ann Street, former executive director of The Greater Middletown Preservation Trust, for

initiating this project during her tenure at the Trust. Our thanks, too, to Trust board members, past and present, for providing help and wisdom along the way.

We would like to thank our sponsors, The Connecticut Light and Power Company, Farmers & Mechanics Bank, Bernie Fields Jewelers, Liberty Bank, Middlesex Hospital, Middlesex Mutual Assurance Company, and Wesleyan University, without whose financial support this book would not have been possible. We are grateful to Pratt & Whitney for providing our sales brochures as an in-kind donation. We also thank our community supporters, who are listed on the last page of this book.

Finally, we would like to thank you, the reader, for making this all worthwhile.

Sharon G. McCormick
Executive Director

A Portland grammar school circa 1910. Seated second from right is Selina M. Brown, who grew up in Portland, but lived most of her adult life in Cromwell. Courtesy Lisa Brown Goldreich

Introduction

By Diana Ross McCain

Envision a stately, mature apple tree. Its trunk is a thick, sturdy foundation from which six boughs of varying lengths and thicknesses branch off in different directions, each growing, twisting into a unique shape.

This apple tree can serve as a symbol, appropriately agricultural, for the history of the six northern Middlesex County towns of Cromwell, Durham, East Hampton, Haddam, Middlefield, and Portland. Each of the six was originally settled—some as early as the mid-1600s, others not until the early decades of the eighteenth century—and occupied for several generations by individuals of similar backgrounds and characteristics: farmers of English ancestry who were devout adherents of the Protestant, usually Congregationalist, faith. They established communities with the family, headed by the father, as the foundation. Within these tightly knit communities there existed a very distinct social ladder. Which rung an individual occupied depended upon such factors as wealth, record of public service, piety, family connections, and personal characteristics. This common cultural origin forms the trunk of the tree.

Eventually, however, the forces of nature, fate, individual personalities, and local, national, and even world events, began to have an impact upon the communities, shaping each one into a unique entity, with a distinctive direction and appearance. These are the six branches of the apple tree.

These forces have varied from town to town in kind, timing, and their ultimate effect upon the individual community. The Connecticut River, so overpowering in size and influence that during the early decades of Connecticut's history it was referred to simply as the "Great River," affected the history of all six towns, even—although to a lesser degree—landlocked Durham and Middlefield. Shipbuilding and trade with population centers along the Atlantic Coast and the West Indies were for decades and even centuries important economic activities in Cromwell, Portland, Haddam, and East Hampton, the four towns bordering the river, while farms in Middlefield and Durham grew produce to be shipped out in that trade.

The extensive swamp between the center of Middletown and the settlement of "Upper Middletown," which made travel between the two so difficult, foreordained that the latter would develop its own identity, and eventually break off entirely as the town of Cromwell. The manner in which several of the other towns were settled determined to a degree the course of their future. The obstacle posed by the Great River made it inevitable that those residents of the original town of Middletown (which was then located on both sides of the river) east of that broad waterway would one day break off and form their own town of Chatham, which originally included both present-day Portland and East Hampton.

The acres of Portland, East Hampton, and Middlefield, also originally part of Middletown, were divided up into sections at various points in time and granted to proprietors of Middletown or their descendants. Settled by individuals who took up residence on scattered plots, they had no physical community centers. Thus it was again inevitable that Portland and East Hampton would split into two towns. Middlefield's lack of a cohesive center kept

it attached to Middletown for well over a century, but it too would eventually secure its independence from the mother town.

Portland, and to a lesser degree Cromwell, endowed by nature with massive exposed outcroppings of brownstone located conveniently close to the Connecticut River, enjoyed a century of prosperity based on the quarrying of that stone which was used for construction both locally and as far away as New York City and San Francisco. The need for brawn to quarry the stone, and the simultaneous occurrence of the devastating potato famine in Ireland in the 1840s resulted in the migration of numerous Irish to Portland, radically changing the nature of the town's economy, religion, and ethnic composition for the first time since its original settlement. In later decades they were followed by Swedish immigrants, who brought yet another language and faith that increasingly diversified the population.

One particular individual, Sylvester Gildersleeve, was the prime mover behind the development of quarrying as a major industry in Portland. Men of extraordinary energy, entrepreneurship, and vision had similar impact upon other towns.

In Cromwell, for example, brothers John and Elisha Stevens started a manufacturing firm that existed for more than a century and became a major producer of iron toys and banks. The need for workers in such factories drew Irish, German, Swedish, and Italian immigrants seeking opportunity in a new land. A. N. Pierson established the first of more than half a dozen nurseries that constituted a major industry in Cromwell, earning it the nickname of "Rosetown," and attracted Swedish immigrants as well. In Middlefield David Lyman II was the moving force behind the establishment and development of the Metropolitan Washing Machine Company, which marketed its product across the nation. He was one of those instrumental in engineering

Middlefield's incorporation as a separate town in 1866 and literally worked himself to death to bring the railroad to Middlefield.

Skyrocketing population growth in the 1700s resulted by the turn of the nineteenth century in a scarcity of land in all of Connecticut, and in real estate prices so high that tens of thousands of the state's young people left in search of affordable land and new opportunities on frontiers from Vermont to California. The population of the six towns, like that of the state, stagnated and even declined for decades and many farms were abandoned. However, new immigrants from countries such as Poland, Italy, Ireland, and Germany, accustomed to poor farmland in their native lands, viewed the abandoned acres of Connecticut as an opportunity, and once again brought them under cultivation.

The history of these communities is embodied most visibly in their architecture, examples of which are featured throughout this book. The "lean-to" house (or "saltbox" as it is popularly called today), found in every town, bears witness to their common cultural origin. The brownstone public structures in Portland are an ever-present reminder of its heyday as a quarrying center. The ship captains' houses in Cromwell, East Hampton, and Haddam recall those towns' days as bustling riverports. The large, impressive homes of such successful industrialists as David Lyman II of Middlefield and Russel Frisbie of Cromwell symbolize a time when manufacturing was a key industry in those communities. The surviving workers' houses are testimony to the thousands of men and women, many new to this land, who actually made the goods that were shipped across the country and even beyond.

This book itself is a distinctive product that has grown from earlier entities. It has used as its foundation the texts developed for studies of the history and architecture of each of these six towns that were produced over the past fifteen years by the Greater Middletown Preservation Trust. All but one of those studies, that for Durham, were published as books, illustrated primarily with photographs of buildings. The success of the Trust's previous book, *A Pictorial History of Middletown*, by Elizabeth Warner, inspired the idea for a similar work for the other six towns embraced within the Trust's geographic scope. The text for each of the original six studies has been edited, updated, and revised to serve as a chapter for each town in the book. The goal of expanding this new book to include more than the architectural heritage of each town led to a search for images that reflect the people who erected and occupied the buildings, who molded and transformed the communities into what they are today.

Long Ago, Not Far Away is a most appropriate title for this work. The men, women, and children who preceded those of us who live in these six communities, whether three years or three centuries ago, are indeed not far away. Their most tangible legacy is their architecture, but they are near us in so many other ways as the words and photographs in this book demonstrate: in the unique physical shape and community character each community has developed, and in the same fundamental human needs, desires, hopes, aspirations, fears, failures, tragedies, and joys that can be seen in the faces of individuals of many different races and ethnic backgrounds that look out at us from these photographs, and whose story is told in the book's text.

We can find ourselves, our common humanity, in each chapter, whether or not we happen to reside in that town, or in any of the six. To read this book will be an experience of both discovery and recognition. We can climb the apple tree's trunk, then venture out upon each of its branches, and perhaps, as we take in the vista of the past and present spread before us, catch a glimpse of our future.

1
Cromwell

Origins 1650–1750

The lands comprising modern Cromwell were originally part of a much larger settlement of the Mattabeseck Indians, obtained by Governor Haynes of Connecticut shortly before settlement in 1650. In 1651 the General Court of the Hartford Colony proclaimed, "It is ordered that Mattabeseck shall bee a Town." In 1653 they "approved that the name of the Plantaytion shall bee called Middletown."

The town's extensive boundaries included a northern settlement called the Upper Houses on a small, valuable piece of

West Cromwell Falls on the Mattabassett River near Pasco Hill Road. Courtesy Middlesex County Historical Society

Tablestone of Rev. Edward Eells, who died in 1776, in the Old Burying Ground. Installed as the second minister in the Upper Houses in 1738, he had served as a chaplain of the Colonial Army and was at the capture of Quebec. Courtesy Cromwell Historical Society

riverfront on the "Great River." The village lay on a small ridge and, although the river was protection against wilderness and Indians, and essential for communications, the small stretch of riverfront placed severe growth limitations on the settlement. South of it, several miles of low meadow and swampland, frequently impassable in spring flooding, separated the northern area from the lower town of Middletown.

The first settlement "was a compact village community," grouped around the present Wall, Pleasant, and South Streets. Each of four settlers—George Graves, Robert Webster, Joseph Smith, and Mathias Treat—was given a three-acre homelot from Pleasant Street east to the river. Nathaniel White's lot was the length of Wall Street. The first inhabitants struggled to secure their survival, and worked to develop a small community on the river's edge, surrounded by thick virgin forest, natural meadows, and swamplands. In a subsistence economy land was their primary asset, and ownership, allotment, and distribution of town lands was important to the early colonists.

All of Middletown's proprietors received land well beyond their needs. Grants made in the settlement area, surrounding land in west Cromwell, and the "East Side of the River" left the settlers land-rich. At his death, John Kirby owned 1,068 acres, David Sage almost 800 acres,

and John Savage had 1,207 acres in 1764.

By the early eighteenth century, the Upper Houses was a small, tightly-knit community, mainly descendants of original settlers. Some immigration and marriages to outsiders brought a steady but limited arrival of new inhabitants. By 1714, the population had grown to fifty householders but there were only twenty family names, suggesting the village's clannish nature.

A Community Emerges

As early grants absorbed the new generations, vacant land dwindled and the expanding population forced the first emigration in the early eighteenth century. As the system of partible inheritance divided family farms into increasingly smaller homesteads, well below the sixty acres needed to support a family, children of the Upper Houses settled in Portland and other surrounding towns.

With increased population, the village organized a school by 1711 and a church (Second Society, being the second Congregationalist Society in Middletown) in 1715, both important steps to define the Upper Houses as a community distinct from its parent town. Middletown and the Upper Houses shared a common government, but the important responsibilities of education and religion assumed by the newly formed "North Society" pulled the upper settlement together and decreased its dependence and ties to Lower Middletown. The first half of the eighteenth century saw an extensive network of artisans within the Upper Houses, including a weaver, tailor, carpenter, tanner, and blacksmith in addition to two gristmills. Separated as a parish, with its own church and school, mills, and small, successful farms, the settlement was becoming self-sufficient and had made the transition to become an autonomous Colonial village.

Riverport Era

As the northernmost deep water port on the "Great River," Middletown developed as the major riverport for the Connecticut Valley with the Upper Houses subordinate in maritime affairs. Following the Revolution and rapid growth in trade, early nineteenth-century Upper Houses had become a riverport whose streets, lined with stylish new sea captains' homes, were busy with shipping, merchant firms, artisans, and shipbuilding, all based on the thriving river trade.

Perhaps the village's increasing prosperity led to a sense of identity and a desire to be independent of Middletown. Late in 1788 a petition went to the Town Meeting from the North Society, Middlefield and Westfield "praying the consent of the Town that they may be established as a distinct town. . . ."

A committee was formed and debate continued until March 30, 1789, when the Town voted "a new proposed Town not be accepted."

Merchants

The generators of Upper Houses prosperity were merchants. Most began as

This house is known as the Wells-Hubbard House on Main Street. It was built between 1795 and 1799. Courtesy Cromwell Historical Society

sea captains, investing in local ships in the lucrative West Indies trade. With luck and judgment many were able to accumulate sufficient capital to open stores supplying a wide variety of imported, manufactured, and fancy goods along with West Indies staples. Frequently these stores procured bulk lots which they sold wholesale.

Only half of a merchant's business was in sales. Many, more properly called merchant traders, purchased farm products for store credit but also quantities of lumber, hay, livestock, or horses for export, either traded to ship captains or shipped to national ports of entry or the West Indies.

Shipbuilding

With two blacksmith shops, a blockmaker, a ropewalk, a sailmaker, and ship's chandlery goods in several stores, the riverport was well able to service its small fleet. A small local shipbuilding industry included a shipyard at the north end of town active in the 1780s. Another on the south end of the village on River Road, south of the Landing, was begun after the Revolution, run by Captain Abijah Savage.

Return to Village Life

Although the War of 1812 began an era of peace and unrestricted movement for American shipping, the Upper Houses reaped few benefits. New York became the East Coast's dominant port and the Upper Houses, with its narrow channel and shoals increasingly unsuited for the larger ships of postwar trade, saw its maritime trade diminish, the merchants it supported disappear, and the Upper Houses decline as a small market center. For almost three decades, the village exhibited little real growth.

Even so, the village's river trade gave it good communication with other urban centers, and supported a good market system. Agriculture remained important, as Cromwell's low meadows, regularly covered by freshets, remained productive even as other Connecticut towns saw their farmlands depleted by generations of farming. The town was generally characterized by tightly-knit family groups with extensive intermarriage and kinship. The church saw several revivals and played a major role in village life. The Baptist Church, founded locally in 1802, grew to rival the prominence of the Congregationalists toward mid-century. In Upper Middletown, like most parts of Connecticut, "the importance of the churches, the family, and the town tended to promote stability and conservatism."

Steamboats

In 1821 William C. Redfield of the Upper Houses was the prime mover behind Cromwell's early involvement in steamboats. He became interested in a steam propulsion system developed by an Upper Houses native, Franklin Kelsey (1793–1861), a talented inventor whose steamboat system had a series of oars driven by centrally-located engines. The

first of these steamboats, built in Cromwell and backed by residents, was "The Experiment," which began regular service between Hartford and Saybrook in July of 1822. The service ended in 1824. Redfield's ensuing involvement with advanced steamboats and commerce on the Hudson River led to his relocation to New York City. Here he was one of the first to envision the overland canal and railroad routes to the West. While transportation was his business, he achieved further prominence as a

William C. Redfield (1789–1857) Courtsey Cromwell Historical Society.

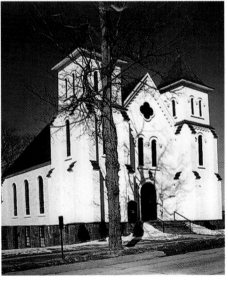

Left: The Methodist Episcopal Church on Main Street was built in 1859. It was purchased and used by the Bethany Lutheran Church from 1910 until 1965. The structure was then demolished and the land is now a parking lot. Courtesy Cromwell Historical Society

Left: The Baptist Church on Main Street was erected in 1853. In 1936 it was sold and became the American Legion Hall. Courtesy Cromwell Historical Society.

21

meteorologist, explorer, and geologist. In 1848 he was the founder and first president of the American Association for the Advancement of Science.

Emigration

Emigration, an acknowledged phenomenon since the Revolution, accelerated as river trade died, markets dwindled, and a whole generation of merchants, captains, shipbuilders and tradesmen sought other employment or left the area. Many went to Hartford, New York, or other cities, but more pushed toward the frontier and there was a steady migration from the village to western lands.

Return to Agriculture

The Upper Houses showed a distinct movement towards agriculture in the first half of the nineteenth century, making the village "rural" in the modern sense. There were many small, efficient farms, but by 1850 tobacco (known since the settlement period) was being commercially farmed with thirteen farmers producing a total of 15,800 pounds of tobacco. These farmers were, almost without exception, wealthy, large landholders, who tended to be community leaders.

Manufacturing and Quarries 1804–1835

The Industrial Revolution, first felt in Connecticut about the turn of the century, made new use of several Upper Houses mill sites with small-scale manufacturing ventures often run on a seasonal basis. In 1804 Frank Franklin, an

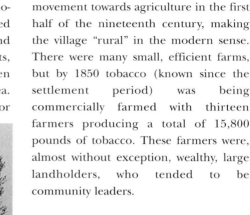

Above: Train rides through the beautiful countryside may seem relaxing to us now, but they were a critical form of transportation before automobiles became commonplace. Courtesy Middlesex County Historical Society.

Right: John J. Monnes was selling milk as early as 1914, taking the name Golden Guernsey Dairy around 1925. Shown in the front seat is Frances Monnes Conroy, with Bernard, John, Ed, and Joe Monnes in back. Courtesy Cromwell Historical Society

Small farms were abundant in Cromwell throughout the years. Pictured is Donald M. Brown feeding his chickens circa 1940. Courtesy Lisa Brown Goldreich

Englishman, established Cromwell's first "manufactory." The Franklin factory spun cotton yarn and stood on one of the several small streams forming Cold Spring Brook, which fed the Sage Grist Mill and sawmill. Another early factory, the Nooks Manufacturing Company, was on Nooks Hill Road a short distance east of Shadow Lane. A small venture, limited probably by market, location and capitalization, it produced candlewick and spinning yarn for the local market. Somewhat prosperous from 1814 to 1823, its production subsequently diminished and ended by the 1830s as a well established factory system in several eastern cities displaced small mills like Nooks.

shifted from textiles to small, finished items. One of the first non-textile industries in Cromwell was hardware. Firms such as Warner & Noble, one of three hammer factories in the village begun in the 1840s, did a steady, prosperous business well into the twentieth century. The first, and for a while, the largest, hardware factory in the 1840s was in the former Franklin factory, refitted as a manufactory with foundry capacity. Run as "North and Savage" from 1839 to 1849 by Edward Savage (an Upper Houses native) and James North, the factory produced a range of miscellaneous cast brass

1835–1860

A dependency on imported raw materials and limited scale of operation and capitalization shaped Cromwell's industry from 1835 to 1860 as production

The J.&E. Stevens Company was best known for mechanical cast iron banks. The "Columbus" bank was designed by Charles Bailey in the late nineteenth century. Courtesy Cromwell Historical Society

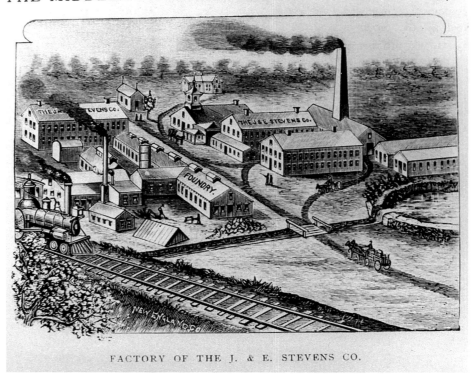

THE MIDDLETOWN TRIBUNE—SOUVENIR EDITION.

FACTORY OF THE J. & E. STEVENS CO.

hardware. By 1874, according to a contemporary map, the building was gone, ending the seventy-year history of Cromwell's first manufacturing site. No trace of the structure survives.

By far the most important business founded in this period was the J.&E. Stevens Company, which came to be Cromwell's largest, longest-lived, and most important company, growing rapidly to surpass any other local industry of the time. Its success was due not only to the variety of objects produced, but the creativity and willingness of its founders to develop new and expanding markets. John Stevens, a native of Bristol, purchased property in the Saddle Hill area of Lower Middletown in 1837 perhaps intending to build in that "industrialized "area. In 1837 and 1838, he also purchased land in the Upper Houses on Nooks Hill Road. He and his brother Elisha began the J.&E. Stevens Company in 1843. Nothing is

known about their first years, but deeds from 1848 show that Stevens erected a new factory building "on the same stream upon which stands the factory and machine shop of North and Savage."

Following construction of this factory, the J.&E. Stevens Company was successful on a scale unparalleled for the Upper Houses. The company's assessed value jumped each year. In 1850, with a capital investment of $16,000, it was the largest industry in town, employing twenty-three men and six women. The company produced many hardware items including shutter lifts and bolts, and door hardware which involved a full range of casting and molding expertise. By 1866, with forty-five employees, it was Cromwell's first modern factory. The factory's most significant items were miniature "toys of various kinds, such as irons, kettles, skillets, stoves, etc." and iron toy wheels, a branch of which later became the company's business. The

This house on Main Street, built by Elisha Stevens in 1863, was the W. R. C. Home for Aged Veterans and Their Wives. Courtesy Cromwell Historical Society

Stevenses formed the "American Toy Company" in 1867, in partnership with George W. Brown of Farmington, an early toymaker and noted designer.

Reorganized in 1868 as the J.&E. Stevens Company with the talented Russel Frisbie as superintendent, the firm began to concentrate on cast iron toys and banks, the earliest of which date to 1869. The company operated a wholesale and retail outlet in New York City, enabling the company to reach and develop a direct market. The Connecticut Valley Railroad, finished in 1871, was a further boon and the Stevens Company prospered for years, closing in the early 1950s.

Quarries

Like Portland, Cromwell has significant deposits of native brownstone. Originally usage of Cromwell's stone was a right of every inhabitant and was the exclusive building stone in chimney stacks and foundations. Unlike Portland, where quarrying took place at "the Ledges" within fifteen years of settlement, in Cromwell there is no direct evidence of

quarrying activity until 1723. The first quarry in Cromwell was "on the Town Commons," evidently on the three square miles laid out to the town in 1671. This public quarry must have been located between Main Street, West Street, and Ranney Road, east of the 1713 cemetery, the site of later quarrying activities. A 1745 reference to "a place called the quarries . . . in the third division . . . in the North Society" establishes that a second quarry was also open, probably west of town center.

By the 1850s rapid expansion of the market for brownstone, aided by arrival of Irish immigrants, stimulated new quarry activity. Several ventures were consolidated as North Middlesex Quarry Company in 1860. The firm's two "free stone quarries" between Ranney Road and Main Street employed 105 men, dug 5,000 tons of brownstone, and had gross sales estimated at $50,000. By 1870 these quarries operated by the "Cromwell Brownstone Quarry Co." produced 10,000 tons of rock worth $150,000, all shipped by boat from lengthy quarry docks along the river. (Spur lines linked quarry and railroad after 1871.) Reorganized in 1892 as the

The Connecticut Brownstone Quarry began in 1852 at the junction of West Street and Timber Hill Road. Producing a very high grade stone, it was a major quarry until 1906. In 1976 it was filled and landscaped. Courtesy Cromwell Historical Society

Connecticut Free Stone Quarry Company, it was for many years a major industry in town, although the "New England Brown Stone Company," organized in 1886, which dug the quarry east of Main Street, was in its time larger.

Growth and Changes, 1840–1860

The decades from 1840 to 1860 introduced considerable changes. Expansion of small local factories and introduction of large-scale quarrying provided many new jobs. For the first time since the early Colonial period, Cromwell's population grew significantly as new immigrants, predominantly Irish in the 1850s and Germans in the next decade, introduced a new range of nationalities and backgrounds into the small New England town. Between 1850 and 1860 immigration changed the town's demography. From a population of 1,259 in 1850, the town grew to 1,476 by 1860. The Irish-born population increased from 12.5 percent to 18 percent (263 individuals). A wave of German immigrants—104 total—came in the same period, forming 7 percent of the population in 1860.

Cromwell had later waves of immigration, notably the Swedish and subsequently the Italians, but these first two, arriving with the rise of the factories and quarries, helped reshape the town's population and economy. As a class removed from the traditional local structure—town, church, community, and land—factors so important in defining the town's character—this group was significantly different from any which had preceded it.

Although the mid-century's new industries enabled a new population to find support, this was a wage-earning, non-propertied class with no lengthy heritage. Little or no record of the Irish and Germans appears in town records. But their labor ran the quarries and factories, renewing the town's economic vigor just before the Civil War; and, as better than one-quarter of the town's population in 1860, they were an important force. As they became assimilated, went through school, purchased property, and rose in local positions, they began to carry influence in community affairs.

The R. O. Clark Brick Yard in West Cromwell opened in 1897 on what is now Sebethe Drive. Men and horses produced forty-five thousand bricks daily until machinery doubled production. Clark's failed in the 1930s, but their bricks are still visible in the Northwest School and the Masonic Building. Courtesy Cromwell Historical Society

The Cromwell Cash Market, circa 1900, was on the east side of Main Street where Ziggy's Barber Shop now stands. It was owned and managed by Walter Bailey, employing John Olson and his son as delivery men. Courtesy Cromwell Historical Society

The MacDonald Store in the center of town was destroyed by fire circa 1900. Courtesy Cromwell Historical Society

Independence

In 1851 the citizens of Upper Middletown made formal appeal to be independent of Lower Middletown. Unlike in 1789, they went directly to the General Assembly with their request. The change they demanded was not great in terms of community, for in practice they had long been distinct from Lower Middletown, but it was great in political terms. Middletown's growth in the nineteenth century made it a modest sized, urban city with important manufacturers and a network of commercial and business affairs. Its large geographical size coupled with its urban-based concerns sufficiently aggravated its differences with Cromwell to open a breach between the two towns, which only increased with the passage of time.

The politics behind Cromwell's move for separation are not clearly set down. But the records—the petition, and meeting proceedings—show that the movement rested its argument on a few simple points:

In their petition for separation, the residents of Upper Middletown specifically claimed that they were not receiving a just proportion of "public money"—taxes, and, in all likelihood, such other revenue as their share of the Town Deposit Fund. They also asserted that their interests were "neglected" by "mismanagement." While the only instance of neglect specified was that the highways were poor, the charge of "mismanagement"—underlined in the petition— was a serious accusation and

Above: The Cromwell Post Office was located on lower Main Street from 1893 until 1926. Courtesy Cromwell Historical Society

Left: George P. Savage, Cromwell's representative to the state legislature, posed with a group of friends on Ladies' Day at the State Capitol in Hartford, circa 1883. Courtesy Cromwell Historical Society

29

clearly grounds for much of the village's dissatisfaction.

Once the petition was drafted, circulated, and sent to the Assembly, separation was apparently almost assured. Then the major issue became what to name the new town. "Cromwell" was the first name proposed, suggested by Rufus B. Sage immediately after the petition was presented and read in March 1851. Few favored the name, more popular ones being Upper Middletown, North Middletown, Middlesex, Auburn, Newport, Glenwood, and so on. The name "Upper Middletown," after several votes, was finally approved at a meeting May 19, 1851, but this name did not stick. The petition to the legislature is said to have had a blank left in place of a name, which was filled in at the last minute with Hamlin, a name earlier proposed by Horace G. Stocking. The call for the first town meeting issued by the legislature shows that by June 16 the name Cromwell had been agreed upon.

It had been 201 years since the first local settlement and in that time, Cromwell had expanded into a farm village, developed briefly as a riverport and market center, and then experienced a decline and quiet period. Now, as its population was reshaped by immigration, as quarrying and manufacturing activities provided a flood of new opportunities, and commercial farming introduced on a widening scale, Cromwell underwent a distinct transformation into a small new town, busy with the vitality of the modern era.

1851–1996

When Middletown Upper Houses assumed its new name and status in 1851 it became Connecticut's 149th town. The initial Town Meeting, with 214 voters, took place in the First Congregational Church on July 16, 1851, and of the fifteen elected officials six bore the names of first settlers. Cromwell then resembled other river towns; maritime trade declining, farming predominant, but with small industries emerging which soon would employ Irish, German, Swedish, and Italian immigrants, it was, with the rest of the nation, poised for growth and change.

Business opportunities grew in the 1870s when railroads offered new mobility and faster shipping for Cromwell's small industries. The Connecticut Valley Railroad started operations in 1871 followed by other state lines. In 1887 the Valley Railroad was leased to the New York, New Haven and Hartford Railroad and sold to that line in 1889; Valley Line

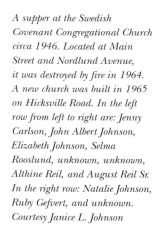

A supper at the Swedish Covenant Congregational Church circa 1946. Located at Main Street and Nordlund Avenue, it was destroyed by fire in 1964. A new church was built in 1965 on Hicksville Road. In the left row from left to right are: Jenny Carlson, John Albert Johnson, Elizabeth Johnson, Selma Rooslund, unknown, unknown, Althine Reil, and August Reil Sr. In the right row: Natalie Johnson, Ruby Gefvert, and unknown. Courtesy Janice L. Johnson

service lasted until 1948 as highways displaced railroads. The New Haven freight depot became Fred Nordgren's hardware store which, recently refitted, serves now as a real estate office and gift shop. In 1871 the Cromwell Bank was incorporated with John Stevens as president, opening in Stevens Hall on Main Street opposite the present office of the Farmers and Mechanics Bank with which the Cromwell Bank has merged.

Andrew Nils Pierson (1850–1925) settled in Cromwell in 1871. By 1872 he had opened Flora Gardens, foreshadowing Cromwell's reputation as a nursery town and paralleling J.&E. Stevens as durable and important industries. When a new strain of roses won a gold medal in 1895 Pierson was hailed as "Rose King" and Cromwell acquired its nickname "Rosetown." A. N. Pierson was incorporated in 1908 and by the 1930s was the nation's largest greenhouse business. Employment at Pierson's attracted many Swedish immigrants, who settled and remain as influential citizens. Andrew Pierson showed concern for his employees and shared his wealth with the town with such gifts as three acres of land and a house for a Swedish Orphanage. The orphanage has evolved into today's Children's Home and

Learning Center. A. N. Pierson's example has been followed through the Pierson's fifth generation of plantsmen and philanthropists.

A. N. Pierson's only daughter, Emily (1881–1970), graduated from Vassar College, Phi Beta Kappa, in 1907. She became an English teacher and an active leader in the women's suffrage movement. After passage of the Nineteenth Amendment in 1920, she entered Yale Medical School graduating in 1924, the only woman in her class. Doctor Pierson practiced medicine in Cromwell for forty years, also serving as town health director and school physician.

The octagon house on Prospect Hill

Above: The New York, New Haven & Hartford Railroad station, circa 1910.

Below: The train and boat landing of the Meriden & Cromwell Railroad on River Road, circa 1886. Brownstone from the nearby quarry was transported from here. Courtesy Cromwell Historical Society

Above: The A. N. Pierson Rose Garden on Main Street was designed in 1915 by Hartford's Elizabeth Park garden designer, Robert Karlstrom from Cromwell. The Pierson Dyer Homestead is in the background. Courtesy Cromwell Historical Society

Right: An early view of workers and oxen at the A. N. Pierson Nursery. Courtesy Cromwell Historical Society

his first automobile. How many additional cars he manufactured remains a question. He next designed and manufactured a variety of superb marine engines, renowned for speed and endurance, that were shipped worldwide from his shop in Middletown.

Some years later Frisbie joined the J.&E. Stevens Company as a consulting engineer and followed his father, Charles Frisbie, as president. He designed some mechanical banks but of greater importance was his repeating cap pistol, more than 6,000,000 of which were sold. He died in 1968, willing his home at 395 Main Street to the Cromwell Historical Society which maintains the 1853 Stevens-

Left: Two Pierson Greenhouses. Courtesy Cromwell Historical Society

was sold to Dr. Winthrop Hallock in 1877 for a "retreat for the nervous and insane." By 1889, under the management of his son Dr. Frank Hallock and later a grandson, Dr. Frank H. Couch and his wife Dr. Mildred Worden Couch, Cromwell Hall enjoyed national recognition for its treatment of nervous disorders. Numerous structures were added and the family was active in town affairs. Closed in 1957, the property is now the campus of the Holy Apostles Seminary and College.

The population had risen to 1,987 by 1890. New building provided space for small stores and services, among them the A. F. Oberg's shoe business which by the 1920s was a popular department store. Farming still flourished and there were five school districts. The Academy was home of the Belden Library organized in 1888 as an outgrowth of the Friendly Association, and honored Josiah Belden, who had donated $1000.

Close to the turn of the century Russell Abner Frisbie (1874–1968) a bicycle racer in Connecticut and Madison Square Garden and proprietor of a bicycle shop, grew interested in automotive engines and purchased the county's first automobile in 1899. Soon he used his design skills at his Cromwell Motor Company at 385 Main Street where he is believed to have built

Frisbie house as its headquarters.

Early in the twentieth century this was still a placid river town. Residents, as in the larger world, did not foresee a century of wars nor the rapid developments in transportation and science. In 1902 the five school districts were replaced by the Nathaniel White School, and in 1911 the Northwest School. Trolley cars came in 1905. There were churches of several Protestant denominations and a Catholic church. Clubs and fraternal organizations abounded. Until 1930 folks enjoyed travel to New York City on Connecticut River steamboats.

Tobacco was always a staple cash crop and introduction of shade-grown tobacco

Delegates to the Evangelical Covenant Church "Summer Conference," August 17–20, 1922, shown in front of the second site of the Swedish Orphanage (built in 1915). Courtesy Cromwell Historical Society

in the Connecticut valley was important in the first half of the twentieth century. Now the nursery town emerged in greenhouses and fertile fields with the Piersons as models. Millane Nurseries and Tree Experts, established in 1913, were the landscapers in 1938 of the Merritt Parkway. They were followed by Leghorns, Casos, Scheus, McNeils, and Gardiners to name a few. Several of these growers are still in active operation.

A 1927 charter authorized Commissioners for a Fire District and a group of Volunteer Firemen. By 1929 they were well equipped and occupied a firehouse. In 1945 the Fire District purchased the Cromwell Water Company.

World War II and the Korean War brought prosperity to Connecticut and to Cromwell. An increasing number of residents commuted to manufacturing plants and Hartford's insurance offices. Many built new homes, patronized local stores and dairies, but also shopped in surrounding urban centers.

Simon Moore, in 1950 the new superintendent of schools, began to modernize curriculum and methods. With completion of a high school in 1958 students no longer traveled to Middletown for secondary education. In 1960 a new elementary school was opened, named in honor of long-time teacher Edna C. Stevens. The opening of Interstate 91 spurred more new housing and the suburban aspect of the town. In 1964, the old J.&E. Stevens buildings became the home of Horton Brasses, known for reproductions of authentic antique hardware.

Cromwell continued to grow during the Vietnam War. In 1968 the first

Below: Seated are Andrew Nils Pierson and his wife Margaret with daughter Emily to the right. Standing, left to right, are sons Wallace R. and Frank A. Pierson (girl in center foreground is unidentified). Courtesy Cromwell Historical Society

Below: Here Russell Abner Frisbie drives a two-cylinder, four-cycle car which he built in 1901. The occasion was the ceremonies opening the Arrigoni Bridge in 1939. Courtesy Cromwell Historical Society.

Top: The octagon house and barn, pictured circa 1883, were part of Cromwell Hall, a well-known sanitarium on Prospect Hill, which operated from 1877 to 1957. Courtesy Cromwell Historical Society

Above: This dormitory, with thirty-one rooms and recreational facilities, was erected in 1908, but was destroyed by fire in 1967. Courtesy Middlesex County Historical Society

Right: This Italianate-style house (shown circa 1896) was built by John Stevens in 1853, and later sold to Russel Frisbie. A circular verandah was added circa 1900. It is now the headquarters of the Cromwell Historical Society. Courtesy Cromwell Historical Society

condominiums, Cromwell Hills, began construction, as well as nearby Cromwell Plaza shopping center. The early '70s building boom gave Cromwell the greatest growth in Middlesex County. Earth Day in 1970 marked the beginning of the environmental movement. Now "green" thinking precipitated conflict over rate of growth and planning and zoning.

In 1973 a new Town Charter increased the number of Selectmen to six, with a First Selectman as chief administrator. In 1975 Lucy Berger was the first woman elected to the enlarged Board of Selectmen. With an enthusiastic celebration of the nation's Bicentennial in 1976 that included a formal commission and support from churches, clubs and schools, Cromwell earned the title Bicentennial Community. This evoked new interest in the preservation of architecture and artifacts as a part of our cultural heritage.

One active and influential Bicentennial Commissioner was Anna Anderson Doering, then president of the Cromwell Historical Society, a well-known piano teacher and for sixty-four years organist and choir director for the First Congregational Church. Elected First Selectman in 1977, Paul Harrington was a strong advocate of commercial development and light industry to enlarge the tax base. One new tax source in 1977 was the retirement community of Covenant Village.

Above: Nellie Oberg and Hilma Anderson await customers circa 1920. Oberg's had the status of an institution, missed by townspeople after it closed in 1964. Courtesy Cromwell Historical Society

Below: Outside the A. F. Oberg Store, with Ella Footit (left), Mr. A. F. Oberg (center) and the Reverend Nilsen of the Swedish Mission Church (far right). Courtesy Cromwell Historical Society

Above: Views of the Nathaniel White School, now the Town Hall. Ruth Buggie Clark was the teacher when these photos were taken. Shown above is a young class in 1925. Courtesy Ruth Buggie Clark

Left: The eighth grade class presented an historical operetta in 1932. Courtesy Ruth Buggie Clark

A young class in 1925. Clark's eighth grade graduating class in 1932, posing in front of one of the Romanesque arches still preserved in the Town Hall. *Courtesy Ruth Buggie Clark*

Built in 1911, the Northwest School was a grade school until 1959, then accommodated other town services. It is currently a private pre-school. Courtesy Cromwell Historical Society

By 1980, with the population topping 10,000, many town facilities needed expansion. A new high school on Evergreen Road opened in 1981, while the former high school became a middle school. With Memorial Town Hall overcrowded, state police and town commissions occupying the former Northwest School and Belden Library crowded into the Academy Building. In 1983 plans were made to remodel the Nathaniel White School building into a town hall and community center. Opened in 1985, the Cromwell Community Center and Public Library is a splendid example of architectural preservation in combination with new construction. The Town Hall welcomed a new administration in November 1985 when Mary Amenta was elected to the office of First Selectman. The town now has more than fifty offices, boards and commissions. A charter change in 1982 established a police force which set up headquarters in the old Memorial Town Hall.

The 1789 ratification of the Constitution was observed 1987–1991, with Cromwell's Commission for the United States Constitution Bicentennial chaired by Elizabeth Bingham. Many programs were at the municipal center where a white flowering crab tree was planted with a commemorative plaque. These local events earned Cromwell distinction as a Bicentennial Community.

The opening of the Connecticut Expressway in 1989 enhanced Cromwell's location at a confluence of busy highways. About 20 percent of housing is in condominiums and apartments in addition to choice wooded enclaves of

single homes, for a population of about 12,500. Shopping centers, other retail businesses, professional offices, hotel and conference centers and restaurants along Route 372 and Route 3 continue to attract non-residents. In 1995 the grand list was $739,685,020.

To the east, not far from the municipal center, Main Street retains its businesses, including three bank offices, while keeping its residential character. The former Edgewood Golf Club has become The Tournament Players Club, site of the annual Greater Hartford Open. In 1994 the State of Connecticut bought nearly 200 acres of upland forest surrounding a

Millane tree experts at work.
Courtesy Millane Nurseries, Inc.

shoreline phenomenon known as the Blowhole and marked it for passive recreation, while Cromwell Landing, two acres of river front park developed by the Rotary Club and other citizens, was added to the town's park system. Both areas lie within the upper reach of tidelands which, from here to the Sound, has been designated as "wetlands of international significance," within the Silvio O. Conte Fish and Wildlife Refuge in the Connecticut River watershed.

Cromwell's variety of homes and lifestyles, educational opportunities, industries, and commercial attractions promote an aura of progress. At the same time there is a certain atmosphere of calm and tradition in the Colonial and nineteenth-century neighborhoods and the recaptured riverfront.

Above: This 1898 view of the rectory also shows a glimpse of St. John's Catholic Church, which was dedicated in 1883. The Church is seen at left enveloped in flames on March 1, 1953— destruction was total. A new edifice on the same spot was dedicated in 1954. Courtesy Cromwell Historical Society

Left: John O. Brown, Sr., first assistant fire chief of the Cromwell Volunteer Fire Department, pictured with a grandson and canine friend "Chips" in 1954. Courtesy Lisa Brown Goldreich

Hal McIntyre (1914–1959), a Cromwell native, joined the Glenn Miller band in 1937, playing clarinet and alto saxophone. In 1942 he formed his own band, one of the twenty most popular "big bands" of the era. He is shown during World War II. Courtesy Cromwell Historical Society

Views of the Armistice Day Parade on November 11, 1922. Courtesy Cromwell Historical Society

Above: This World War II air raid warning post was manned by members of the Carlson-Sjovall Post of the American Legion. Bottom right: This 1944 photo shows Company F of the Connecticut State Guard, composed of men from Cromwell and East Hampton. Courtesy Cromwell Historical Society

CROMWELL HONOR ROLL

ANDERSON, HARRY J.
ANDERSON, ALBERT E.
ANDERSON, CARL A.
ANDERSON, THOMAS E.
AUSTIN, MILLARD B.
ABEL, HELEN
ABEL, JESSIE T.
BARROWS, CADELLA I.
BEERS, ROWLAND T.
BLAKELY, FRANCIS L.
BLAKELY, SILVESTER W.
BINKS, A. ERNEST
BOGUE, LINWOOD I.
BRIGGS, WALTER G.
BUTLER, RALPH S.
BUTLER, SYLVESTER B.
BURKHARDT, MARY
BOGUE, RALPH
CARLSON, ADOLPH V.
CHRISTIANSON, CARL F.

CLARK, HAROLD T.
★ COUCH, EDWARD S.
★ CARLSON, EDWIN E.
DAHLEN, CARL AXEL
DOWLING, DANIEL
DOWLING, JOSEPH
DUTTON, PHILO G.

EAGER, GEORGE
EWALD, JOHN E.
EWALD, MARTIN
EWALD, ROBERT
EWALD, ALFRED D.
FILLMORE, LESTER A.
FILLMORE, MILLARD E.
FOOTIT, JOHN D.
FOSTER, JESSE J.
FRAZER, WILLIAM H.
FREGIRI, LUIGI

★ GULSTRAND, EDWARD
HAZELWOOD, STEPHEN M.
HJATT, IRVING P.

HALLOCK, AVERY A.
HALLOCK, LEONARD A.
HILDRETH, EARL W.
HUBBARD, HORACE S.
HEDLUND, BENJAMIN
JOHNSON, ARTHUR A.
JOHNSON, CARL A.
JOHNSON, EDWIN W.
JOHNSON, GEORGE

KABATZNICK, MORRIS
KAISER, CHARLES
KEENAN, JAMES
KLINE, JOHN W.
LARSON, VICTOR
MAGNUSON, SAMUEL
MARGUILLI, SETTINO
MARIOTT, LEON
McLANE, OSCAR W.
MEE, JOHN H.
MERRILL, WESLEY P.
MEYERS, FRANK
MACKIE, GORDON

NELSON, FREDERICK
NIELSEN, LAURENCE
NIELSEN, OSCAR
NOBLE, KENNETH M.
NOBLE, LEROY B.
HIGHBERG, AXEL L.
HIGHBERG, CARL J.
OLSON, CARL W.
OLSON, WALLEN T.
OSTERGREN, CARL H.
OSTERLUND, OSCAR

PEDERSON, MARTIN C.
PETROFSKY, JOSEPH G.
PIERSON, PAUL N.
PROUDMAN, ISAAC

★ RANNEY, PAUL W.
REIMAN, WILLIAM
REIMAN, FRANK A.

SJOVALL, ARVID H.
SJOVALL, JOSEPH
SJOVALL, HERMAN
SMITH, GEORGE
SWANSON, CARL A.
SWANSON, HAROLD

THORELL, CARL
TOSCO, JOSEPH
TRAVIS, WILLIAM H.
TUVESON, ERNEST W.

VINBLADH, JOHN A.
VINBLADH, CARL W.
WYER, STANLEY
WATKINS, MYRON J.
WATROUS, ALDEN S.
WHITNEY, VERNON F.M.
WOIKE, JULIUS C.
WYNINGS, ROYAL W.
YOUNGBERG, EDWARD
ZENS, AUGUST

This World War I Honor Roll stood on the Upper Green until the dedication of a memorial to all World War Veterans in 1925. Older photograph courtesy Cromwell Historical Society, newer photograph courtesy Bernadette S. Prue

The Cromwell Branch of the American Red Cross provided extraordinary support during World War II. Mrs. John O. (Selina) Brown was head of that Chapter. Courtesy Lisa Brown Goldreich

Report Given On Red Cross Work In Year

Large Amount of Surgical Dressings Completed By Small Group.

CROMWELL

CROMWELL, Nov. 23.—The surgical group, Cromwell branch of the Red Cross, celebrated its first anniversary last evening. The class met as usual at Cromwell hall and during the evening a report was made of the accomplishments of the past year. A total of 30,600 dressings have been made in 3,363 hours. There are over 100 registered for this work but only 42 of these women are active workers. Service bars for one year's service and over 100 hours have been earned by the following: Mrs. David Nyren, Mrs. Arthur Rhodes, Mrs. Paul Turner, Mrs. Peter Madsen, Mrs. Elsa Carlin, Mrs. Frank Olson, Mrs. Charles Johnson, Miss Elizabeth Brown, Miss Gertrude Steffins, Mrs. Gustaf Carlson, Mrs. Oscar Larson and Mrs. John Brown. Many others will receive their bars in December. A number of members have earned production pins for 75 hours service and almost all of the volunteers have earned Red Crosses for 18 hours.

The dressings are made, inspected, tied and packed in bags and then sent to Middletown to be put into cartons and shipped. Cromwell is noted for its quality work.

The class was organized under the able direction of Mrs. Thurston Johnson assisted by Mrs. John Brown. Last May Mrs. Johnson resigned to join her husband in Virginia and Mrs. Brown was named chairman, and ap-

pointed Mrs. David Nyren, vice-chairman. They are assisted by the following supervisors: Mrs. S. Arthur Rhodes, Mrs. Peter Madsen, Mrs. Paul Turner, Miss Elizabeth Brown, Miss Doris Haddock, and Miss Ann Lindquist.

This work is a great humanitarian task that must be done and it is hoped that after the holidays more of the women of Cromwell who have registered in the past year will find time to attend classes once more.

After the class, a party was held at the home of Mrs. David Nyren. A beautiful birthday cake, surrounded by red roses and topped with a lighted white candle was presented by Mrs. Howard Mart and a cake decorated with a white ground and red crosses to represent the chairmen and supervisors and workers was made by Mrs. Charles Johnson. Many other delicious refreshments were served and a delightful social hour was enjoyed.

An important meeting of the building committee of the American Legion will be held this evening at 7 o'clock, preceding the regular meeting of Carlson-Sjovall Post at 8 o'clock.

The Boy Scouts will meet this evening at the Legion hall at 6 o'clock.

Enjoy your Thanksgiving dinner at the Casino Grill, Boston Post road, Saybrook, $2.50, children $1.50. Make reservations early.—adv. 2411

Court St. Cecelia, C. D. of A., will hold a harvest card party this evening, at the K. of C. hall. The public is invited.

The annual Thanksgiving service of the Covenant Congregational church will be held Wednesday evening at 7:30. A special program will be featured and the customary "Thank-Offering" of a day's wages will be received for the local church expenses.

Mrs. William Post

Mrs. Louisa Post, of Main street, widow of William Post, died this morning at the Middlesex hospital, after a short illness. She leaves a

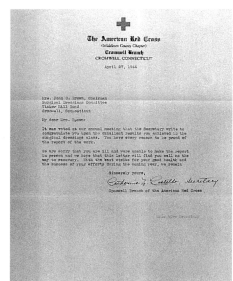

✚

The American Red Cross
(Middlesex County Chapter)
Cromwell Branch
CROMWELL, CONNECTICUT

April 27, 1944

Mrs. John O. Brown, Chairman
Surgical Dressings Committee
Timber Hill Road
Cromwell, Connecticut

My dear Mrs. Brown:

It was voted at our annual meeting that the Secretary write to congratulate you upon the excellent results you achieved in the surgical dressings class. You have every reason to be proud of the report of the work.

We are sorry that you are ill and were unable to make the report in person and we hope that this letter will find you well on the way to recovery. With the best wishes for your good health and the success of your efforts during the coming year, we remain

Sincerely yours,

Catherine L. Luttle, Secretary
Cromwell Branch of the American Red Cross.

This young class is shown outside the Center School at its original location on Prospect Hill. Courtesy Cromwell Historical Society

Children of the South District School, also known as the Bell School, are shown circa 1900. The building was remodeled into a private home in 1902. Courtesy Cromwell Historical Society

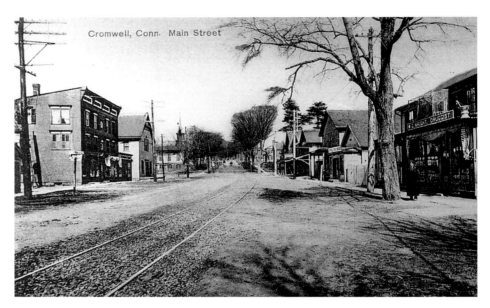

Cromwell, Conn· Main Street

Top: A postcard view of Main Street. Courtesy Middlesex County Historical Society

Above: The Campfire Girls' Indian Float in the Patriot's Parade on July 4, 1918. A thousand people took part in the mile long march. Courtesy Cromwell Historical Society

Left: This Victorian-style house later became the home of Anna Anderson Doering, the well-known historian, musician, and civic leader. Courtesy Cromwell Historical Society

In the early age of the automobile, Charles A. Johnson's garage did business on the east side of Main Street. Courtesy Cromwell Historical Society

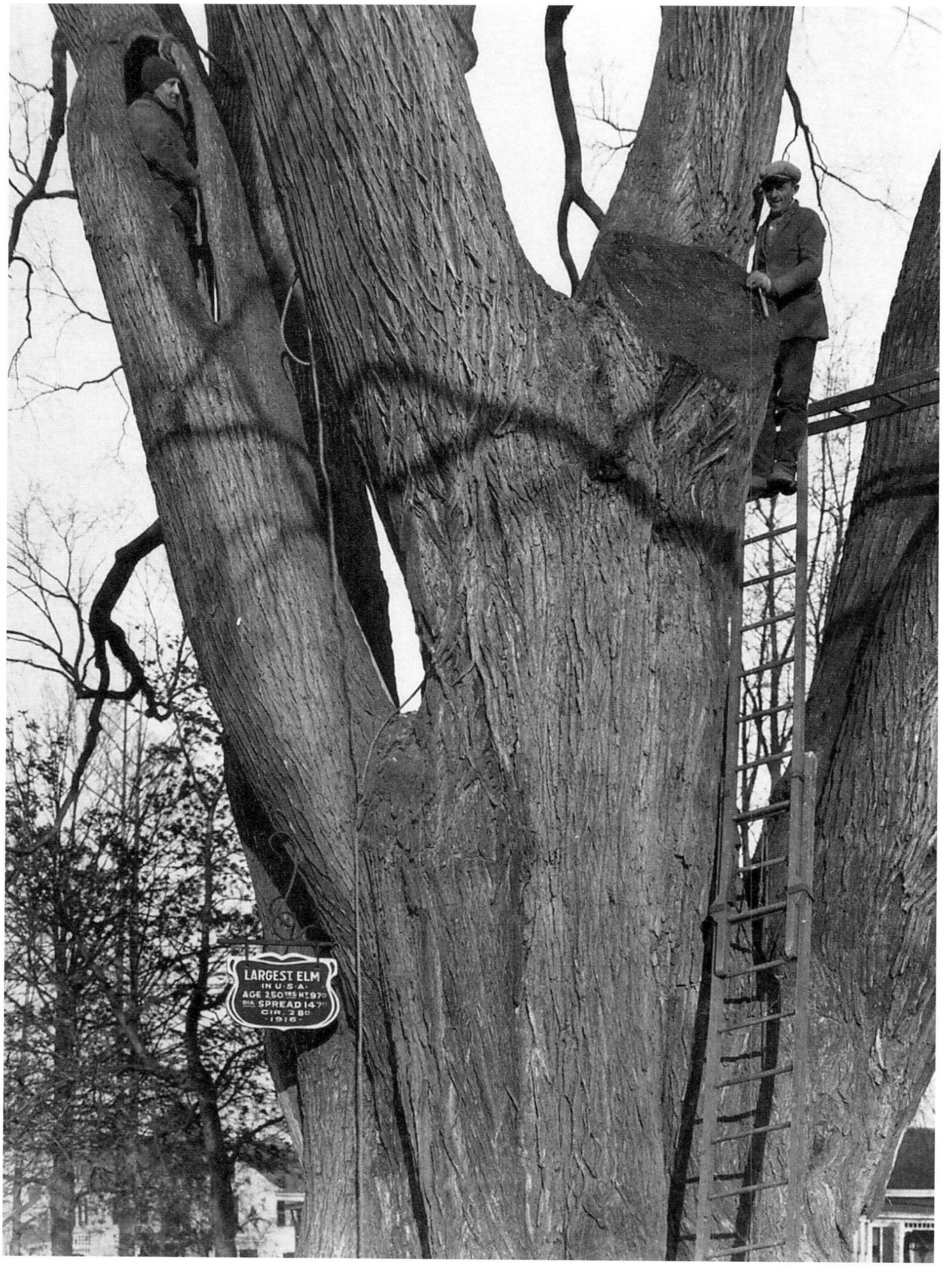
LARGEST ELM
IN U.S.A.
AGE 250
SPREAD 147
CIR. 28
1916

The largest elm tree in the United States circa 1916: 250 years old, 97.5 feet high and 147 feet spread. Courtesy Millane Nurseries, Inc.

Right: Local gas stations included Dorman's, Kincaid's, Newberg's, and Frank's, circa 1947. Courtesy Cromwell Historical Society

Below: Views of the Connecticut River flooding on March 21, 1936. Courtesy Cromwell Historical Society

Above: The center of town looking south. Courtesy Janice L. Johnson

Below left: Looking north at the intersection of Main and West Streets. Courtesy Cromwell Historical Society

Above left: Rowing down Wall Street. Courtesy Cromwell Historical Society

2
Durham

Durham Settlement

Durham (Coginchaug) was established relatively late in the seventeenth century by the third or fourth generation of Connecticut settlers. Its rugged topography, extensive swampland, and rocky ledges discouraged even the Native Americans from settling here. Moreover, it had no access to the sea. The Connecticut Colony was settled in organized townships of groups of proprietors to whom the General Court granted lands sufficient for immediate needs, and for those of future generations. Population growth, immigration, and partible inheritance led to a

Main Street looking toward Middletown, taken from Maiden Lane. Courtesy Durham Historical Society

53

The Street — Durham has one street

Wishing you all a Merry Christmas and a Happy New Year. Fondly, Mary, R.

"Durham has one street" according to the notes on this postcard. Courtesy Fran Korn

rapid diffusion of family and community land resources in southern New England through the second half of the seventeenth century. By the 1690s younger inhabitants of established settlements were anxiously looking for somewhere to set up their own homesteads. Not surprisingly, a good many began to look to Coginchaug.

By the 1690s the General Court had granted most of the land in the area to individuals and Coginchaug belonged to an assortment of absentee landowners from Hartford, Saybrook, Guilford, and Branford. In 1699 the Court granted a petition to incorporate Coginchaug as a township; a committee was appointed to lay out the town plat. The Guilford faction, dominant at first, wanted it laid out in the southern part of the town to enhance the value of their properties. Such a plat was laid out by the committee in the fall of 1699. But the powerful Hartford interests prevailed upon the General Court to relocate the town center to a place more advantageous to their property values. Not until 1703 was it relocated to its present site, on lands owned by the heirs of John Talcott of Hartford.

The organization of the plat itself appears to have engendered little controversy once its location was established. The committee of the General Court chose to follow the plan used in Middletown and Hartford—with the homelots along a central "Great Street" rather than around a central green. Durham's "Great Street" (sometimes referred to as "the King's Highway" in early deeds, but more generally called "the Main Street") ran from the Wadsworth Place, south of the present Green, to the present intersection of Main and Route 147. Paralleling this were two smaller streets, the "Back Lane" (now Maple Avenue) and another to the east of Main Street (now Brick Lane and Cherry Lane). Land was set aside for the support of the ministry and for a corn mill and sawmill on Allyn's Brook. By 1708, when the grant of incorporation, the Durham Patent, was issued by Governor Saltonstall, thirty-four families had taken up residence. In 1722 the town set land aside for its first schoolhouse. By 1756 the population was 1,076.

Colonial Durham, 1708–1776

William Chauncey Fowler, in his History of Durham (1866), accurately summarized the character of life in Durham before the American Revolution

54

with the phrase "there were family government, family instruction, family amusement and family religion." The rights and freedoms of early Durhamites were not the prerogatives of individuals but of heads of families. New England laws required that all individuals live in households under the authority of the head of a family. This was the basis of the social order, for the head of the household was entrusted with the duty not only to maintain order among his own dependents but also to provide them with the rudiments of literacy, religious instruction, and vocational training.

It was common for children of both sexes, even from well-to-do families, to be bound out as apprentices in the homes of their neighbors to learn farming, house-keeping, and the artisan crafts. These extended families were the center of social and economic life. Faced with the difficult task of subduing an uncultivated wilderness, members of the town's households from early childhood were engaged in a seasonal round of activities devoted to providing food, clothing, and shelter. Housing—barns, outbuildings, and the homestead itself—was a continuing process of building additions to contain growing families and herds, as well as an endless task of maintenance.

More important was the problem of fuel. Every family had a woodlot and every able male cut and split wood to feed the voracious hearths. A typical household required between eighteen and thirty cords of wood annually, all cut by hand.

Top: This photograph shows Hubbard's Hall on Maple Avenue and the Quarry School, one of the town's earliest schools, on the Wallingford Road (Route 68). Courtesy Fran Korn

Bottom: Wellman's Corner, taken April 1, 1909. Courtesy Durham Historical Society

Above: J. Petrosky and H. I. Page are shown with their wagon and two yoke of oxen, on Main Street in front of the Methodist Church. Courtesy Fran Korn

Below:Benjamin Wysocki and his oxen team on Main Street in front of the Town Hall. He worked for the Lyman Farm in the early 1900s. Courtesy Emily Wysocki

Land use was important. Woodlots supplied timber and cordwood. Flax yielded linen to make clothes. The men planted, harvested, and beat the flax, the women carded and spun it for the men to weave. Wool, too, was an important source of material for clothing.

Production of food was also a central concern. Staple grains like wheat, corn, and rye were planted, harvested, and ground into flour and meal at the gristmill on Allyn's Brook. Durham's marshes produced hay. Cows provided milk, butter, and cheese, hides from which shoes were made, as well as tallow for candles and lamps. Oxen hauled heavy loads and moved stones from fields, and, eventually, became the basic ingredient of savory roasts and soups. Poultry supplied eggs, feathers for bolsters and mattresses, and an occasional meal. Orchards provided fruit and the woods, too, offered a bounty of maple sugar. Every household member had particular responsibilities. Many skills were assigned to men—husbandry, hunting, and woodcraft, shoemaking, metalworking, milling, tailoring, or weaving—who passed them on to their sons. Daughters tended to housekeeping, spinning, knitting, and sewing for the household.

The family also played a role in the larger life of the community. The heads of families were the basis of political and religious authority, and were often the only ones in the household who could vote in town matters. All were required to attend church, but being admitted to communion was a far more selective affair, contingent on the collective judgment of the community, which meant the heads of households. Thus, while Durham's early inhabitants enjoyed freedoms unknown to their ancestors in the Old World, those freedoms were circumscribed by a pervasive structure of family authority.

Finally, the families of the community were informally ranked in terms of a deference order. Certain families, the Talcotts, Wadsworths, and Chaunceys, for example, dominated the political and ecclesiastical life of the town, serving year after year as justices of the peace, representatives of the General Court, selectmen, officers of the militia, and deacons of the church. Some families had a near monopoly on certain offices: for example, Wadsworths, father and son, served continuously as town clerks from 1707 through 1786. The ministry was no different: for 126 years, from 1706 to 1832, the spiritual affairs of the community were overseen by the Chaunceys. In early Durham the family itself stood within a greater family, overseen by the fathers of the town.

Durham Architecture, 1708–1765

Of the 102 structures shown on the 1765 map of the Durham, only thirty-three

Above: The Durham Town Hall. Courtesy Fran Korn

Below: This old cemetery still exists near the Mill Brook Bridge on Main Street. Courtesy Fran Korn

Town Hall, Durham, Conn.

OLD CEMETERY, DURHAM, CONN.

remain standing—all considerably altered. Of the 132 structures shown on the James Noyes Wadsworth map of 1827, only seventy-two survive, fifty-two of which were built before 1800. The thirty-three houses built between 1708 to 1765 represent five basic patterns of residential architecture. By far the most common early housing type is the two-and-a-half story five-bay central chimney structure. Of the fifteen pre-1766 houses of this type in Durham, thirteen possess gable roofs. Two others, the Elnathan Chauncey House on Fowler Avenue (c. 1755), and the Elnathan Camp House at the corner of Main Street and Maiden Lane (c. 1758), have gambrel roofs.

Some houses of this type have been so altered as to be almost unrecognizable; such alterations, although changing the

character of the structures, are of architectural merit in themselves and signal the remarkable ability of Durhamites to adapt older structures to changing styles. Among the best preserved and least altered examples are the Ithamar Parsons House (1733–1734) and the Merwin-Southmayd House (before 1737) at the corner of Haddam Quarter Road and Oak Terrace. The second early housing type is the two-and-a-half story three-bay central chimney residence, of which several examples survive, among them the Samuel Fenn Parsons House on Main Street (1708–1714).

The third type is the five-bay central chimney saltbox structure, five of which survive. These houses represent a transition from an early one-room deep structure with an added lean-to to the more common two-and-a-half-story houses. This transition was complete by the time Durham was settled, so all of Durham's saltboxes were built as such, with integral rear lean-tos. They include the David Baldwin House (1722–1733) at the corner of Foothills and Haddam Quarter Road and the Fairchild-Merwin House (1727) page 59 near the intersection of Haddam Quarter Road and Brick Lane.

The fourth housing type is characterized by a gable end which faces the street, the façade containing either three or four bays. The three extant structures date from the 1730s: the David Robinson House (before 1735) on Maple

Avenue, the Roberts-Moffitt House (1739), and the Jonathan Walkley House (1733–1778), both on Main Street.

The fifth housing style is the Colonial Cape, a one-and-a-half-story central chimney structure often surmounted by a gable roof. A good example is the Hill-Spelman House (1730) on Main Street, which boasts a number of atypical elements including a gambrel on the front portion of the roof and a saltbox lean-to at the rear.

Sources of Change

Durham's "Great Street" was one of the major intercolonial roadways, so the town was exposed to external influences and ideas; many of its inhabitants made their livings serving the needs of travelers. Durham was close to Middletown, which was, by the 1750s, becoming a major port from which New England's agricultural surplus was shipped to the Caribbean. Tied to the outside world, Durham was not immune to the political and religious turmoil that would, by the 1770s, culminate in the movement for American independence. Internal factors also forced changes. Families grew faster than the town's limited reserves of arable land

could support. Its market orientation encouraged the migration of the young out of farming and, as lands became available in western Massachusetts and New York, out of Durham. The first signs of change began to emerge in the 1740s in connection with the Great Awakening.

The Great Awakening was a religious

Top: Located on the Haddam Quarter Road, this house was built for Samuel Fairchild in 1727. It was subsequently owned by Miles Merwin, the founders of Merriam Manufacturing Company, and the Durham Academy. Courtesy Durham Historical Society

Above: This building on the corner of Main Street and Wallingford Road was restored by the laymen and laywomen of the United Churches of Durham in 1991. The Church was awarded the Greater Middletown Preservation Trust Bufithis Award for the quality of the restoration. Courtesy Bernadette S. Prue

Left: Newton's Hotel catered to many travelers that passed through town. Courtesy Fran Korn

59

Above: John Swathel purchased this tavern in 1802. It was located on the corner of Middlefield Road and Main Street (where Dairy Mart is now), and was one of the most popular taverns in town. Unfortunately, once their children were grown, his wife Phoebe went insane and had to be kept locked in the attic because of her violent fits. Painting Courtesy Rev. Augustine Naduvilekoot, Notre Dame Church

Right: This old engraving of Durham shows the second and third Congregational Meeting Houses. Courtesy Jim Sarbaugh

revival which pitted the forces of reform against the established churches, causing deep divisions in New England society. The reformers, or "New Lights," favored an emotional return to anti-establishment religious experience. The "Old Lights" represented the established Congregational Church and were appalled by the perceived excesses and spiritual passions of the reformers. The "New Light" preachers lured their congregations from the established church to become Baptists and, later, Methodists; this rift in religious orientation was a serious blow to traditional Congregationalist ideology.

Although the Great Awakening had a profound impact on Durham, it had small power against the forces of population growth and land scarcity, economic transformation, and political upheaval. The Revolution revealed a fundamental split in the town. Some families, like the Goddards and the Chaunceys, were Tories, the former so flagrantly against the

Revolution that their property was confiscated and they were forced into exile. Elihu Chauncey (1710–1791) walked a tightrope between respect for established authority (which included the King of England) and the new nation's struggle for independence. He refused to take the "oath of fidelity" to the Revolutionary cause, required of all public officials, and was forced to resign from the legislature and the Superior Court, but he avoided arrest, confiscation of his estate, and exile.

Durham, like all of Connecticut during the Revolution, suffered the loss of family members, the deterioration of farms, and the immense economic burdens of inflation and taxation. After the war, the town began to change in obvious ways. The deferential political order was fast disappearing, as old families like the Chaunceys and Wadsworths were politically discredited and others, once submissive to their "betters," assumed authority. After decades of stable political power based on land, new men, many of them merchants and craftsmen—Guernseys, Parsons, Scrantons, Camps, and Butlers—began to be elected with regularity to public office.

The rise of political conflict paralleled a breakdown in religious unity. For some years, the Congregational Church under the leadership of Elizur Goodrich, who had assumed the pulpit in 1756 on the death of Nathaniel Chauncey, had attempted to ameliorate the strains on Durham's religious community. A liberal, Enlightenment-influenced clergyman, Goodrich was not afraid of new ideas and was willing to meet religious skepticism in the spirit of rational argument. As long as he lived, the Durham Church held together. But on his death in 1797, the religious community disintegrated. Many were drawn towards the more intense services of the Methodists who were, by the mid-1790s, gathering adherents from throughout the greater Middletown area. Artisans, especially shoemakers, were frequently drawn to the new sect, although its numbers also included wealthy farmers like David Lyman. The Episcopalians, although based in Middletown, were also attracting adherents, especially from among the more wealthy and politically conservative inhabitants.

The breakup of religious unity was accelerated by the efforts of the established Congregational Church to recapture its straying members. On Elizur Goodrich's death in 1797, the Deacons of the First Society recruited a young Calvinist zealot, David Smith, to serve as minister. He and the Deacons began a purge of backsliders in 1801 and by 1806 eighteen members had been expelled. By 1808 the Deacons and Smith turned their attention to community morality in the larger sense: they banished the practice of attending balls. But these efforts affected only those who remained in the church and even among them, it left a heritage of bitterness that would, by the 1830s, result

First Church of Christ, Durham, Conn.

Left: The First Church of Christ, built in 1847 with lavish Greek Revival ionic columns, was the fourth congregational meeting-house erected in Durham. Courtesy Fran Korn

Below: One of the local church school groups on an outing. Courtesy Durham Historical Society

The Church of the Epiphany, shown here in 1906, was built in the mid-nineteenth century in the Carpenter Gothic style. Courtesy Fran Korn

The original First Church is now part of the United Churches of Durham. Courtesy Bernadette S. Prue

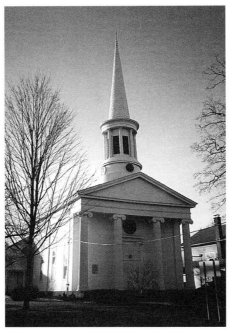

in a breakup of the First Society and the unseating of the zealous Reverend Smith.

Durham Architecture, 1766–1830

The houses built in Durham between 1766 and 1830 reflect both the changes and the continuities in its social and economic life: the breakdown of cultural and religious unity and the increasing orientation to the market economy. The eighteen houses built between 1766 and 1799 exhibit remarkable diversity. While all but one of these houses were built as central chimney structures, only four retained the classic two-and-a-half-story, five-bay configuration. These include the Deacon John Johnson House (c. 1780) on the Guilford Road and the Samuel Hart House (c. 1780) on Stage Coach Road. Of the three three-bay, two-and-a-half-story structures built during this period, only one harked back to earlier building traditions—the Jeremiah Butler House (c. 1775), almost an exact copy of the Samuel Fenn Parsons House (1708–1714) on Main. The other three-bay houses, the Henry Crane House (c. 1785) on Cherry Lane and the Center School (c. 1775) on the Green were far more modest in their proportions. The most common house type built during these years was the ordinary Cape, of which five were constructed. These include the Jesse Cook House (c. 1772) on Main Street and the Wilson-Clark House (1777–1778) at Haddam Quarter and Foothills Roads. In contrast to these unpretentious houses, the residence built by Thomas Lyman IV on the Middlefield Road in 1778, looked forward to a new world of prosperity and individualism. It is a Georgian-style structure, with two chimneys and a central hallway.

Finally, the period 1766 to 1799 marked the appearance of structures built for purely commercial purposes. Traditionally, Colonial families lived and worked under the same roof. But an important component in the development of the modern lifestyle was the separation of workplace and residence. The Squire-Bates Store (1796) on Main Street, for example, was built adjacent to the residence of Daniel and Guernsey Bates, the storekeepers.

Between 1800 and 1830, a period of continued religious, economic, and political unrest, Durham's architecture showed few signs of innovation. Only by the 1820s did a national style from the aesthetic mainstream, such as the Greek Revival, begin to appear. As before, the two-and-a-half-story five-bay center chimney house remained dominant, representing six of the twenty-three houses built between 1800 and 1830. Many of these, like the Squires-Scranton

House (c. 1800) and the Lemuel Camp Tavern (1806), both on Main Street, were substantial, but extraordinarily conservative architectural statements, their only concession to their times being the addition of Federal-style porticos.

Above: The Jesse Cook House later came to be known as Mill Hill. It is now a private home located beside the Post Office. Courtesy Fran Korn

Left: Down the road toward Middlefield with the Lyman homestead in the background (close to the current Apple Barrel Store). Courtesy Durham Historical Society

Left: The Gaylord Newton House exemplifies the early architecture of Durham, with its central chimney and two windows on either side. Courtesy Durham Historical Society

Above: This early view of the Durham Market shows three Greek Revival houses to the right. This area was highlighted in the historic district ordinance of the town. Courtesy the Durham Market

Right: This cluster of Greek Revival homes was located at the merge of Maiden Lane and Main Street. It was the largest concentration of this style of homes on Main Street. Courtesy Fran Korn

Maiden Lane from Main St., Durham, Co

Curiously, only five houses during this period were built in the Federal style, characterized by delicate and restrained classical ornament and by leaded glass fanlights.

The first and most notable house of this type to be built in Durham was construct-ed in 1803, appropriately for the Rev. David Smith. The house stands on the Green and shows many Federal characteristics, including a delicate classical portico, a finely wrought fanlight, and the first side-hall floor plan of any house in Durham.

Nineteenth-Century Durham

Confronted with new spiritual, political, and economic challenges, the town became oriented to market agriculture, as the rutted roads between Durham and other towns were rebuilt by private investors as turnpikes. Durham became a nexus for three private roads, including the important New Haven, Durham, and Hartford Turnpike, which improved on the old "Stage Road" of Colonial times.

In market farming, too, there was money to be made in clever speculations in commodities and land. Cattle from upstate New York were brought to Durham, either to be sold to West Indies traders from Middletown or to be taken to the slaughterhouse, located to the south of the bridge over Allyn's Brook. Most of the meat was salted and sold as provisions for ships sailing out of Middletown and other nearby ports. The hides were processed in the tanning yard (also on Allyn's Brook)

and were sold for use in the growing local shoemaking industry.

Most remarkable was the pattern of diversified activity among farmers that emerged in the late eighteenth century in which agriculture was combined with trade and commerce. While households were able to combine farming with mercantile speculation, most chose the simplest alternative: keeping the family farm intact, usually for the youngest son, promoting the out-migration of another, and training the rest as craftsmen, usually as shoemakers.

New markets and occupations opened a range of economic and cultural opportunities that would have been unimaginable in an earlier age. By the 1820s, as the journal of Mary G. Camp (1799-1841) indicates, young Durham women of moderate means could be fully as cultured and refined as their counterparts in Hartford and New Haven. Miss Camp, the daughter of taverner Lemuel Camp, was educated at a private female seminary in Litchfield. By the 1820s Durham could boast a lyceum, an organization where

Left: This dapper young man with his horse and buggy was photographed on July 3, 1888. Courtesy Middlesex County Historical Society

Below: Courtesy Fran Korn

The pleasure of your company with Ladies, is requested at the

SOCIABLE,
—GIVEN BY—

THE Y. M. S. C.

LEACH'S HALL, DURHAM, CONN.,
Thursday Evening, January 29th, 1885.

Music by Merrill's Orchestra.   Edward Clark, Prompter.

TICKETS,   -   -   -   ONE DOLLAR.

townspeople gathered to debate issues of public interest, and hear touring lecturers on literary and scientific subjects. There was also an increased investment in the public schools, which were organized on a district basis in the 1830s.

But the transformation of the town from isolated self-sufficiency to market participation also brought real social costs. Durham ceased to be a community in which the inhabitants invested time and energy in the common good. People now looked first to their own interests, encroaching on common lands, litigating and contending against one another. A more serious issue was the social fragmentation resulting from the increasing importance of the crafts. The crafts had the virtue of permitting one to stay in the town where one was born, rather than venturing westward. By 1820 Durham was no longer overwhelmingly a farming community and by 1850 the occupational composition of the town had become more complex and the differences in wealth more pronounced: of the 280 households containing individuals with listed occupations, 127 were farmers, 51 were laborers, 44 were shoemakers, 10 were joiners, and the remainder followed a variety of callings.

Many skilled crafts—tailoring, for example—were eliminated by competition or became obsolete. To be a craftsman in

Durham had come to mean, almost without exception, to be a shoemaker. And after the 1820s this meant struggling for survival in an intensely competitive market increasingly dominated by merchants who extended credit, provided the raw materials, and controlled the markets. Accordingly, the shoemaker declined from a relatively prosperous and independent craftsman to a mere wage earner. After 1840 only a few hardy individuals remained in the shoe trade, the most successful of whom was Bennet Beecher. His establishment (which still stands on Main Street) was the last large-scale shoe operation in the town. But even he eventually failed. The company dissolved in 1864, ending Durham's connection with the leather industry.

Durham Architecture, 1830–1870

While Durham's architecture between 1830 and 1870 presents considerable stylistic variation, it demonstrates far more aesthetic coherence than the houses built between 1766 and 1829. The new styles were derived from the emerging aesthetic mainstream reflecting a national, rather than local, identity. There was now a far greater degree of stylistic uniformity. Of the sixty surviving houses built in Durham between 1830 and 1870, fifty were built in

The Post Office was located for a time across the street from its present location. This building is now a Grange Hall. Courtesy Fran Korn

This "Tin Shop," photographed circa 1905, reflects the need for small handcraft businesses along with the larger industries. Courtesy Fran Korn

Top: This lovely lady is obviously ready for a parade with her horse and buggy. The photograph is dated July 20, 1909, but she is identified only by the initials B. R. Courtesy Fran Korn

Above: More fun than walking when the snow gets deep (mailed November 30, 1908). The scene is on Main Street in front of the Durham Academy. Courtesy Fran Korn

Left: Mrs. Minnie Nettleton Halleck and her husband lived in the Sabbath Day House on Indian Lane. Courtesy Fran Korn

The interior of the Methodist Episcopal Church was lavishly decorated. The banner reads "God is our Refuge and Strength." Courtesy Fran Korn

The Ladies Aid Float from the Methodist Episcopal Church, October 3, 1917. Courtesy Fran Korn

two styles, the Greek Revival (28) and Nineteenth Century Domestic (22). The remaining ten were either atavisms: Federal (4), Cape (2), or Georgian-Colonial (1); or oddities Italianate (2) and Carpenter Gothic (1). The stylish houses (Greek Revival, Federal, and Italianate) tended to be built either for the well-to-do or as public buildings, whereas the Domestic Vernacular structures tended either to be modest homes or small commercial structures.

The public buildings constructed in Durham during this period—Methodist Episcopal Church, Grange Hall (1836), Durham Academy (1843–1844) and North Congregational Church/United Churches (1847)—tended to carry the full range of

Greek ornament. Both Congregational churches carried grandiose temple-form facades, while the Academy and the Methodist Church/Grange Hall were ornamented more modestly.

Within a few years other Greek Revival residences were constructed, among them the Henry Tucker House/Congregational Parsonage (1838), the William A. Parmalee House (1839–1842), and the Robinson-Andrews House (c. 1840), all on Main Street.

The next most popular style in Durham during the years from 1830 to 1870 was the nineteenth-century Domestic or Domestic Vernacular style. In most instances this style incorporated the structural features of the Federal and Greek Revival, with the gable end facing the street and a side-hall floor plan. Its lack of ornament pretended to nothing more than Yankee practicality. Twenty-four buildings of this type were constructed during the middle decades of the nineteenth century, two of which were schoolhouses (the North and South District Schoolhouses on Main Street and on Sand Hill Road). Three were stores or industrial structures such as the Henry Davis Store (c. 1851) on Main Street. Of

the sixteen Domestic-style residences, half were extremely modest one-and-a-half-story structures such as the James Hinman, Jr. House (c. 1835) on the Wallingford Road and the Andrew Jackson Robinson House (1836) on Maple Avenue. By the late 1850s, however, the Domestic style was winning acceptance by Durham's wealthier citizens. These more luxurious renditions of the style tended to be far more commodious than their humble predecessors: they were usually two-and-a-half stories and often enlarged by rear or

Above: An interior view of the North Congregational Church circa 1907, showing elaborate holiday decorations. Courtesy Durham Historical Society

Left: This home, locally known as Harvey's Corner, was at the intersection of Main Street and Wallingford Road. Courtesy Fran Korn

The District School is shown here with teacher Ruth Gladwin and an early class. Courtesy Fran Korn

The Walkley summer house, built in the Italianate style, was razed when Notre Dame Catholic Church was built. Courtesy Fran Korn

side additions. Examples are the Henry M. Coe House (1859) and, more particularly, the handsome residence of Francis Hubbard, Merriam Manufacturing Company president, both on Main Street.

The Italianate and Gothic Revival styles were not popular in Durham. Only three Italianate houses were built: the Wentworth Wadsworth House (1855) and the Leverett W. Leach House (1867–1868), both on Main Street, and the now demolished Webster Walkley House, on the site of Notre Dame Church.

Post-bellum Durham

The Civil War changed the character of the town. Its population, which reached 1,130 in 1860, began to decline steadily, hitting a low of 884 in 1890 and not recovering its 1860 level until 1930. Manufacturing declined and the quality of rural life began to deteriorate. The collapse of Durham's agricultural base and the depletion of its population, however, opened the town up to new influences and new people. Immigrant farmers from Ireland, Germany, Italy, and Poland, accustomed to poor farmland in the Old World, looked to Durham as a promised land. They eagerly purchased Durham farms at low prices and restored them to production. The Italians had a particular attraction to agriculture. Some of these families had emigrated, worked in industry or in the building trades, and then came to Durham. Other immigrant families, like the Arrigonis, started out in Durham in semi-industrial activities—in their case the production of charcoal—and then moved on to construction, contracting, and agriculture. But these were not the only newcomers to Durham. There was an increasing influx of "summer folk," people from Hartford, New Haven, and other nearby cities who purchased farms as vacation homes.

Durham benefited from other aspects of modernity. The advent of the automobile and the paving of Route 17 contributed to its growth as a suburb of Middletown. With this development, it became possible to separate the character of the town from its economic base, for by the turn of the century Durham was becoming fully integrated into a regional context.

By the 1890s Durham was beginning to pull itself out of the decline it had suffered since the end of the Civil War. The organization of the Durham Grange in 1887 and the Durham Fair Association in 1893 were signs of the revival of agricultural morale. The public library was

Above: This fancy three-story house, built in 1865, was originally home to Francis Hubbard. It was later owned by F. F. Brewster. Courtesy Durham Historical Society

Middle: The Durham Consolidated School, known today as the Frank Ward Strong School, was constructed in 1923 as part of an upgrade of the town's educational system. Courtesy Fran Korn

Below: The 1937 graduating class of Durham High School. In the back row from left to right are: Edith Leining, William Leining, Alice Moush, Al Saltus, Irma Scaglione, and Tom Suchaneck. in the front row are: Norma Pratt, Rod Libby, Serafino Pandiani, and Jeannette Stannard. Courtesy Bernard and Irma Scaglione Prue

Right and Below: This building was constructed in 1851 by Henry Canfield as living quarters and a wagon factory. The earlier photograph with automobiles shows the area in 1937, courtesy Fran Korn. Known today as Ackerman's General Store, it is shown in the newer photograph courtesy of Ackerman's Store.

Middle right: Enjoying grapes at the Arrigoni Brothers Vineyard. Courtesy Fran Korn

Right: Flocks like these provided meat, feathers, and eggs in abundance. Courtesy Fran Korn

completed in 1902, the public school on Main Street in 1923. The willingness of the citizenry to contribute their capital to the rebuilding of the Merriam Manufacturing Company (destroyed by fire in 1918) and to underwrite the establishment of a new firm, the Durham Manufacturing Company in 1922, were indicators of the commitment of Durhamites to the town's survival. By their actions during the period from 1890 to 1930, the townspeople were acknowledging their participation in a larger universe of politics, culture, and economics.

Durham Architecture, 1870–1932

The town's buildings during the years from 1870 to 1910 were remarkably uniform. The practical, unpretentious, and economical Domestic style was overwhelmingly favored. By the 1870s balloon-framing, the construction of house-frames from standard-dimension milled lumber, came into common use, greatly reducing the cost of construction. Moreover, the invention of practical small steam engines made the use of power tools almost universal in the building trades by the 1870s and significantly decreased labor costs. And finally, changes in domestic technology also played a role in this

Above: Durham Fair—oxen pull.

Middle: That's quite a kale he's holding. George Stevens, age ninety, won first place for this vegetable entry at the 1946 Durham Fair.

Below: The Merriam Manufacturing Company entered this float in a Durham parade. Courtesy Fran Korn

stylistic shift. Iron heating stoves reduced the amount of masonry needed for chimneys and burned fuel much more efficiently. These new economies made it possible for persons of modest means to maintain houses of considerable size.

Houses in the Domestic style tended toward two basic forms, one influenced by Federal and Greek Revival traditions, the other by Victorian fashions. The former and by far the most common favored overall structural symmetry and gable-to-street orientation. They were, in essence, temple-form houses without classical ornamental references. Examples include the John A. Fowler House (1872) on Fowler Avenue and the Canfield-Parsons House (c. 1880) on Main Street.

The Victorian influence on the second major Domestic style variant expressed itself in the massing of the structure. Victorian styles favored asymmetrical,

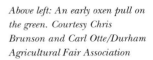

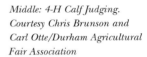

Above left: An early oxen pull on the green. Courtesy Chris Brunson and Carl Otte/Durham Agricultural Fair Association

Above right: Leroy Brock poses with two sets of twin calves born of the same dam (center) during the 1958 and 1959 Fairs. Courtesy Chris Brunson and Carl Otte/Durham Agricultural Fair Association

Middle: 4-H Calf Judging. Courtesy Chris Brunson and Carl Otte/Durham Agricultural Fair Association

Below: Girls do more than sew and cook. "Trained steers of Miss Leonard of Cheshire" is the identification of this photograph in the fortieth anniversary "Gold Book" of the Fair. Courtesy Chris Brunson and Carl Otte/Durham Agricultural Fair Association

Above: Abner Roberts and his cattle in action. Charlie Wimler of Durham provided the equipment to move the heavy loads back into position. Courtesy Carl Otte/Durham Agricultural Fair Association

Below left: This State Police Emergency truck is shown in front of the Atwell House, once a private home, but now the year-round administrative offices for the non-profit, all-volunteer Durham Fair AGricultual Fair Association. Courtesy Carl Otte/Durham Agricultural Fair Association

Below right: Abner Robers and Mr. Ferrell are shown with Abner's cattle. Courtesy Carl Otte/Durham Agricultural Fair Association

Above left: "The Old Elm" was among the largest of the few remaining large elms in the state when this photograph was taken. Courtesy Fran Korn

Above right: The original Mill Brook bridge, shown here in three views, was rediscovered beneath the current roadway during recent repairs. An award winning design for the new bridge allows viewing of the original bridge as seen in the third view. Courtesy Fran Korn

Middle: Courtesy Durham Historical Society

Below: Courtesy Bernadette S. Prue

irregular masses. Thus a fairly straightforward temple-form Domestic structure like the Methodist Parsonage (c. 1895) on Main Street might deviate from symmetry through the incorporation of a small, two-story gable-roofed addition, a feature also seen in the H. D. Daniel House (1904) on Haddam Quarter Road. Self-consciously fashionable Victorian houses include the Andrew Hull House (1877–1878) on Main Street.

The economic and social changes affecting Durham left few obvious marks on its architecture. Certainly rural abandonment took its toll on the town— but its primary architectural manifestation was the deterioration and razing of houses from the colonial period. The selective prosperity of the time is evident in the proportion of handsomely stylish houses to the mass of undistinguished plain Domestic style structures, especially modest rental properties like those built for the Merriam Manufacturing Company workers on Maple Avenue. Of the immigrant groups only the Italians made a distinctive mark on the town's housing. They had a pronounced preference for masonry structures, a preference that would be expressed at first modestly, as in

Twin Pine Farm house and barn represent the small farms which flourished in the area, supplying dairy, egg, and vegetable products to customers in the surrounding towns. Thomas Lyman probably built the original portion of the barn in 1785. Charles Parsons later purchased the farm and built the house in 1854. Mrs. Augustus Otte sold the farm to Alessandro and Pietrina Scaglione in 1927, when these photographs were taken. Courtesy Bernard and Irma Scaglione Prue

Below right: The Mill Pond Dam was essential in creating the right flow of water for the mills along the brook. Courtesy Durham Historical Society

Below left: Typical farm countryside. Courtesy Middlesex County Historical Society

the handsome brick Dutch Colonial Revival Arrigoni House at the corner of Guilford and Meeting House Hill Roads and in the assortment of brick and stone structures comprising the Naples Farm on Bear Rock Road. The style reached its ultimate expression in "Graystone," the remarkable estate laid out by the Arigonis on Blue Hill Road in 1942.

The erection of the Durham Library in 1901 in a very real sense marks the dividing line between the town nineteenth- and twentieth-century architectural sensibilities. Although notable as the first structure in Durham to be designed by an architect, as well as for its neo-Classical design, it is also the first public building in town in which the style clearly differentiated it from both residential and commercial structures. This distinction became more explicit with the construction of the neo-Classical Durham Public School in 1923 and the Durham Volunteer Fire Company Engine House in 1932.

Residential structures built in Durham after 1910 also show an unmistakable departure from eighteenth- and nineteenth-century building traditions. Beginning with the Willis I. Parmalee House (1909–1910) on Parmalee Hill Road, Durham dwellings abandoned all regional reference and were drawn entirely from the national architectural mainstream.

Like the Colonial-revival houses, the bungalows built in Durham in the 1920s and 1930s suggested a yearning for a rural past which was neater, cuter, and less complicated than the past which Durhamites had actually experienced. At the same time, it expressed a cultural and aesthetic nationalism that had first emerged with the Greek Revival style in the late 1820s, but was not fulfilled until a century later when the same kinds of houses were being built across the country, inhabited by people who shared the same aspirations, consumed the same brand-name commodities, read the same newspapers and magazines, and crowded around their radios, much as their ancestors had clustered by their hearths.

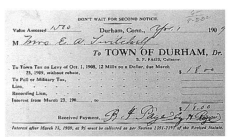

Above left: Dr. E. A. Markham and friends. Courtesy Durham Historical Society

Top of page: An order receipt from W. A. Parsons & Company. Courtesy Fran Korn

Above middle: A tax bill from the town of Durham to Mrs. E. A. Twitchell. Courtesy Fran Korn

Left: The Atwell sisters. Courtesy Fran Korn

Below: Sunday best and then some! Courtesy Durham Historical Society

Top left: Mrs. Hunt on her 106th birthday, mailed on August 31, 1906. Courtesy Fran Korn

Top right: Taken at Mary Stone's hundredth birthday, April 28, 1965, at Durham Convalescent Home on Brick Lane. She was involved in the first Durham Fair. Helping out is Elizabeth (Betsy) Hall. Courtesy Carl Otte/Durham Agricultural Fair Association

Below: A fine day of shopping and good fun. Courtesy Fran Korn

increased by 328 percent from 1700 to 1730. But either the shortage was less acute in Middletown or the land east of the river was considered of very poor quality, for the proprietors were slow to exploit their eastern landholdings.

Early settlements sought parish rights once sufficient numbers of people had arrived. Ecclesiastical societies were established so that settlements distant from the town center could attend Sunday worship more conveniently. Once a community had enough people, it would petition the state for a separate parish. Acknowledgment as a separate parish exempted the members from paying taxes to the central church and occasionally conferred other privileges such as municipal improvement of the roads that gave access to their new meeting house.

Before 1714 any resident on the east side of the river had to attend church in Middletown proper. In 1714 the Third Ecclesiastical Society of Middletown was granted. The petitioners for this parish apparently all lived within the present bounds of Portland. The first portion of East Hampton to break off from the Third Society parish was the southeastern corner

which was incorporated as part of Westchester parish. In 1739 East Hampton's second parish was established. This society, Middle Haddam parish, included the present Middle Haddam section of East Hampton and all of Haddam Neck. East Hampton parish, the last parish established in eastern Middletown, was formed in 1746.

In the early eighteenth century, the eastern residents began lobbying for a separate town. In 1767 a petition was submitted to the Connecticut Assembly. Called Chatham, it was granted township with the limitation that there be only one representative from the town to the

Above: The Deacon West House was built in 1745. Courtesy Chatham Historical Society

Left: Middle Haddam Library at he corner of Route 151 and Knowles Road. Constructed as a store in 1799, it was leased to Cyrus Bill and Daniel Tracy. Seth Overton replaced Tracy, and the store became known as Bill and Overton in the early nineteenth century. It was converted to the Herd home between 1815 and 1825. In 1908 the property was sold to the Library. Courtesy Chatham Historical Society

Area Civil War veterans in 1865. Courtesy Chatham Historical Society

General Assembly. Local tradition asserts that this name, the name of an English shipbuilding town, was chosen because of the shipbuilding activity along the riverbank in Portland and Middle Haddam. Chatham was also the name of a large Cape Cod town, near Eastham, the origin of a number of East Hampton settlers, which may have been a factor in the name's selection. Since Chatham was composed of three parishes that had developed independently of one another it had no inherent center. Not long after its establishment, movements were underway for further municipal subdivisions. Further details concerning these subdivisions can be found in the Portland section of this book. Chatham was renamed East Hampton, the name of the 1746 parish, in 1915. That East Hampton was divided into hundreds of privately owned strips meant that its settlement would be directed by arrangements between individuals rather than by a community plan. This is reflected in the decentralized nature of the town today.

Middle Haddam

Middle Haddam is on the east side of the Connecticut River, six miles south of Middletown. Its greatest concentration of historic architecture is at Knowles Landing, a stretch of river frontage that was the center of local commerce and industry between 1780 and 1830. Development of Middle Haddam began in the 1720s, both in the Hog Hill/Chestnut Hill region and at the landing. Hog Hill, the first area to be settled, centered around a ridge about a mile southeast of Knowles Landing. Only a few remain of the thirty-eight houses that were here in the mid-nineteenth century. Although the area had been divided among the Middletown proprietors as early as 1674, settlement did not occur until over fifty years later. The development of this land in the third and fourth decades of the eighteenth century coincided with a land shortage in Connecticut. The land had been depleted by poor farming and timbering methods by that time.

The parishioners erected a church on Hog Hill in 1744. Middle Haddam residents sought permission from the town of Middletown to build a pound for stray livestock in 1743. Nearby was a pesthouse where people would go to weather initial stages of smallpox inoculation.

It would be a mistake, however, to imagine this community as an integral village organized around the church, or as an eighteenth-century prototype for Knowles Landing. There was no common land as a point of reference for dense settlement. Middle Haddam parish was comprised instead of individually owned farms spreading from present-day Cobalt down to Haddam Neck, with Hog Hill the approximate center, and therefore the most convenient place for a church.

Early settlers were farmers, but maritime activities played a part in their lives from an early date. Boats were built on the river in the mid-eighteenth century and there were other river-based enterprises. By the time of the Revolution, a number of Hog Hill residents were sufficiently familiar with seafaring to go to war on ships. The lure of the sea played a role in the decline of Hog Hill's importance. For the survivors of the war, the increased awareness of the world and experience gained from being in the navy must have made them consider the advantages of sailing over farming. Upon their return, many shifted their sights from Hog Hill to Knowles Landing.

Easthamites were a large faction in the settlement soon after 1738. They pursued limited shipbuilding and trade in the early years in addition to farming. This seafaring inclination spurred development of Middle Haddam as a riverport. With a ready population of skilled sailors and shipbuilders, Knowles Landing quickly became a mercantile center of importance disproportionate to its size. The focus of Middle Haddam shifted to the Landing, or more precisely, the once diffuse community developed a center. And for Easthamites and their descendants, farming on Hog Hill diminished in importance as seafaring, which had always been an avocation, became a feasible livelihood.

By the late 1720s, before any settlement of the Knowles Landing area had been recorded, it was established as a small docking and manufacturing outpost for Middletown entrepreneurs. Jonathan Yeoman, who built his house next to the

river on the landing, is the most significant initial settler. In 1732 Yeoman obtained a right to erect a gristmill on Mine Brook next to the sawmill; in 1741, he also built a gristmill on Pine Brook to the east. In 1735, he received a license from the General Assembly in Hartford to establish a ferry across the Connecticut River from the landing to the Maromas section of Middletown. Actively cultivating the land he owned, Yeoman had established an orchard at the landing by 1741. Development of the landing proceeded slowly but steadily over the next several decades, and included both an increase in cultivated lands and the expansion of commercial activities.

The arrival of Joseph Parke in about 1758 was significant in the development of the village. Hailing from Groton, Connecticut, Parke was skilled as a cooper. Quickly procuring an interest in the gristmill on Mine Brook, he utilized his skill at making hogsheads to export flour and other goods from the area.

The church and other social institutions of the community were still located on Hog Hill. As no records remain which describe the activities of the Knowles Landing area in these years, it is difficult to assess the degree to which the riverport had developed into a trade center for the farms which were established in Middle Haddam and East Hampton by 1775.

The Revolutionary War provided an opportunity for developing the maritime

Cobalt Railroad Station on Depot Hill. In 1908 East Hampton voted to provide transportation by rail between Cobalt and East Hampton for Middle Haddam scholars attending school in East Hampton. Passenger service was discontinued in 1927 and school train service in 1931. The tracks were put into use again in 1936 after the hurricane washed out roads. Tracks from Cobalt to Columbia were torn up in 1966. Courtesy Chatham Historical Society

capabilities of Middle Haddam residents. It spurred the adventuresome spirits of both seasoned captains and young recruits and exposed greater numbers of these seamen to the opportunities and wider commercial networks available in the large ports. Furthermore, a few local merchants fared well financially through their privateering efforts.

There was another influence working during the Revolutionary War period which served to expand the scale of shipping and industry in the Knowles Landing area. That there was a significant deposit of minerals underneath Great Hill in Cobalt had been known since the early 1660s. An early governor of Connecticut, John Winthrop, was granted title to this land which was believed at that time to contain gold. In 1771 mining operations began on Great Hill to extract cobalt ore from the ground by a crew composed of foreigners who apparently had little interaction with the locals, so that few details remain to inform us of the nature of this operation.

During the two decades following the Revolutionary War, the Knowles Landing community fully established itself as the commercial center for a wide inland area to the east. One important sign of the development of this area as a village center was the construction of the Episcopal Church in 1787. Prior to this, religious services in Middle Haddam had been observed in the Congregational Church on Hog Hill. Following the Revolutionary War, this church suffered a declining enrollment. The Anglican Church established at the landing, on the other hand, seems to have been well supported from its inception.

The merchant community experienced rapid growth through the 1780s and '90s. By 1790, three of these companies sold imported goods from Europe and the West Indies primarily to farmers who lived in their region. The goods included fabrics, shawls, gloves, and other dress goods, as well as books, kitchen utensils, and tableware, window glass, bar iron, and other items. Foodstuffs which could not be produced locally, such as tea, coffee, spices, and chocolate, were also available.

Farmers sold their surplus produce to the merchants at the landing, who either shipped them to their suppliers as payment for the salable goods they had received, or traded them on the open market for cash or other merchandise. Marketable goods known to have been shipped from the landing in this period included oats, potatoes, onions, hay, salted fish, beef, pork, shoats, horses, lumber, and barrel staves.

From the mid-1780s, another important Middle Haddam export was distilled rum. Importing molasses from an outside source, refining it, and reselling it on the export market, freed merchants at Knowles Landing somewhat from dependence on the limits of agricultural production in the region. Furthermore, the value of manufactured products exceeded that of farm goods, thereby increasing the profits from each shipment.

As the national beverage of the period, rum was in great demand in virtually all markets. Indeed, New York merchants relied heavily on Connecticut for their supply of domestic rum. Distilling did not require a large labor force or a high level of expertise, but it did require large amounts of firewood to keep the boilers operating. Because wood was far more accessible in outlying areas such as the Connecticut Valley than in large towns such as New York, it was profitable for city merchants to support the distilling operations of small villages.

It is likely that Middle Haddam merchants were directly involved in the "coasting trade" (trade with New York and other Atlantic seaboard ports as opposed to trade with foreign ports) from the 1770s through the end of the century. This trade would have been stimulated by the establishment of the distilleries at the landing.

Whether merchants at Knowles

Landing engaged in direct traffic to the West Indies in the 1780s is not clear. From the beginning of the Revolutionary War through the 1780s, the British kept West Indies ports closed to American shipping, and trade from Connecticut to this region was severely curtailed. In 1793, however, hostilities broke out between the British and the French, which required the British Navy to turn its attention back to Europe. The lifting of this blockade brought a fast return of American trade to the area.

While there were dangers involved in commerce with the West Indies, there could also be substantial rewards. Middle Haddam merchants traded actively and directly with the West Indies after 1793. Two or three vessels were employed from Knowles Landing in this trade during the mid-1790s. By the end of the decade, there were about five boats sailing directly from the landing to this area. Income from the

West Indies in the 1790s, combined with the coastal trade and distilling operation, produced the first real money seen in Middle Haddam. One sign of this wealth was the expansion of docking facilities at the landing. During the 1790s, there were at least four separate wharves constructed along the waterfront.

The architectural character of the village also underwent an important change in this period. In the late 1790s, several stylish and contemporary homes

Cobalt Intersection, Route 66 heading west toward Portland, circa 1935, courtesy Chatham Historical Society. Note Rubin Ostergren's Esso gas station on the right and Cobalt Market on the left. The same area is shown in 1996, courtesy Bernadette S. Prue

These members of the Middle Haddam Rifle Club won the Nutmeg Rifle League Trophy in 1927–1928. Courtesy Chatham Historical Society

were erected. Three domestic buildings, finished in late-Georgian and Federal styles, began a trend toward contemporary styling which was followed by virtually every property of consequence which was constructed after this time.

The final and probably the most important development of the landing area in the 1790s was the establishment of the commercial shipyards. Prior to this time there were some boats constructed here but no property had been actively developed for the exclusive purpose of shipbuilding. Not until investment capital had been accumulated, and skilled craftsmen had arrived in the area, did this industry begin to operate on a large scale.

The shipbuilding industry maintained the village's prosperity in the wake of mercantile success. Commercial shipbuilding allowed Middle Haddam

entrepreneurs direct access to the developing mercantile economies of larger centers, especially New York. Far more than rum, manufactured ships were a product which was in demand by merchants in these trade centers. In the large ports, waterfront land for wharf space was at a premium, and locally produced timber was scarce. Merchants in the larger towns and cities were eager to buy ships produced in outlying communities, and were willing to pay high prices for them.

Shipbuilding in the Nineteenth Century

Commercial shipbuilding at Knowles Landing began in 1797 when master carpenter Thomas Child purchased a piece of land on the Connecticut River and established a shipyard. In 1799 master carpenter Daniel Tracy purchased property and established a second shipyard. His operation, however, proved to be unsuccessful and was sold in 1806. From 1797 to 1800, ten vessels are known to have been constructed at the landing, and from 1801 to 1805, another twenty-two. Some of the schooners constructed here were probably kept by local merchants and used in coasting and West Indies trade. But even in the first years, the business was characterized by an emphasis on the construction of large ships, to be sold to merchants of large coastal ports engaged in international trade.

A number of notable vessels were built in Middle Haddam. The whaling ship Alexander, built in 1821, sailed out of Nantucket, making trips of several years in length, including a four-year tour of the Pacific. The ship Sarah, another whaler, was among the largest boats built here: 122 feet long with a cargo capacity of 501 tons.

Skilled craftsmen were required for precise sawing, joining, trunneling, making fittings, caulking, and painting. Five years after its inception, the shipbuilding industry was sufficiently established to attract laborers and craftsmen from a wide area. Gradually the more specialized ship artisans took up residence at Knowles Landing.

While it is common knowledge among present residents that Middle Haddam was a shipbuilding village, the scale and nature of the operation has not been generally understood; shipbuilding was the primary enterprise that generated the architectural environment which remains today. While the industrial evidence must be reconstructed from accounts, land records, and recollections, many of the houses built during the shipbuilding era still stand. Middle Haddam's architecture continued to reflect a progressive influence through the 1820s.

Four homes built during this period reflect the Federal style and three, by their gable-to-street orientation, foreshadow the Greek Revival temple form. A conservative trend set in during the following decade, however. While Middle Haddam can boast nine houses from the Greek Revival period, nowhere in Middle Haddam do we see examples of the Greek Revival style which are comparable to those beginning to develop in East Hampton.

As suggested by the architecture, the shipbuilding industry, which had been the sustaining force during Middle Haddam's period of growth (1800–1830), was beginning to decline in the 1830s. There was a concurrent lull in house construction. Middle Haddam shipbuilding owed its decline to a number of factors. Raw materials were harder to come by as the intensive shipbuilding and lumber exporting of the previous decades had depleted the forests by the 1840s. The natural limitations of the river were also a problem. The labor supply was drawn from elsewhere. Local laborers became involved in small-scale manufacturing in East Hampton. In fact, the decline of shipbuilding coincides with the development of industry in East Hampton and a consequent shift of activity from the riverport to the mills nearby on Pocotopaug Stream in the center of town.

Shipbuilding resumed on a much smaller scale later in the century. The last three vessels built at the Middle Haddam yards were three-masted schooners. The Gerti M. Rickerson built in 1884 was the last boat ever launched here. Other small industries developed in Middle Haddam in the mid-nineteenth century: iron forging, production of trunk trimmings and rollers, grinding of feldspar, manufacture of metal to line bearings, and manufacture of silk ribbon and toys.

Aside from this small-scale industrial activity, Middle Haddam became primarily a residential community in the wake of shipbuilding. It was home base for sea captains, yet their business interests were generally centered elsewhere. Their children often kept these houses as summer retreats. In the last quarter of the

In 1936 the Connecticut River flooded Middle Haddam and its Dock House. Courtesy Chatham Historical Society

nineteenth century, Middle Haddam became increasingly a resort community. Summer tourists arrived at the landing by steamer from New York and later by railroad direct to Cobalt Depot.

Although the Connecticut River steamers continued to operate, making stops here until the 1930s, the river declined as a significant transportation artery. The arrival of the railroad in 1874 rerouted much of the former trade; the Air Line Railroad passed about a mile north of Knowles Landing. Middle Haddam remained accessible but insulated from the mainstream of economic activity. Thus there was very little residential

development during the first half of the present century. The community appealed to people by its very remoteness, however, and a number of New York families bought older houses here, to escape the heat and bustle of the city during the summer. Middle Haddam inhabitants never lost sight of its natural and architectural resources. For this reason, a remarkable array of historic houses remains.

Damage in Middle Haddam from the 1938 hurricane. Courtesy Chatham Historical Society

East Hampton Center is shown looking south circa 1900. A trestle crosses over Main Street and Siebert's Opera House is in the background. Courtesy Chatham Historical Society.

East Hampton: Settlement and Early Farms

Main Street, East Hampton has been a focus of town activity throughout its history. Settlers naturally gravitated to this location southwest of Lake Pocotopaug because of its natural advantages. In the eighteenth century its agricultural potential was exploited and in the nineteenth century, by virtue of its proximity to Pocotopaug Stream, it proved to be a focal point for the development of the bell industry.

Between 1740 and 1743 there was an influx of settlers to the area. There was initially no central point in town around which settlement clustered. Lots were narrow horizontal strips stretching about a mile east to west and from fifty to several hundred yards north to south. Much of the soil in a given lot might be unsuitable for farming so a settler would often consolidate several lots to accumulate a workable farm, and settlement tended to be more concentrated in agriculturally productive areas.

There was an early clustering of houses along Main Street, most of them built by farmers. In 1750 the Congregational parish voted to build a meetinghouse. It was erected in 1752 on the corner of Summit and Main Streets, west of Pocotopaug Stream. In 1757 the parish voted to establish a school which was built in 1761.

Farming was the primary occupation of East Hampton's first settlers and continued to employ the majority of the townsmen until the late nineteenth century, well after the establishment of local industry. East Hampton farmers were producing primarily for their own consumption with some surplus for export out of Middle Haddam. The chief products were Indian corn, wool, and livestock. Other grains, such as rye and buckwheat, were produced to a lesser extent, but wheat, destroyed by a blight in the 1770s, was never a major crop after that time. The forests also were an important resource for farmers, providing lumber for houses in addition to barrel staves and ship timber. Goods for export, while never the mainstay of East Hampton agriculture, were nevertheless important in shaping the town's economy as they linked each farmer with distant markets, thereby creating an awareness that was a prerequisite for later industrialization.

After 1797 when Middle Haddam's shipyards became established, East

Hampton men were also involved in shipbuilding there, providing both labor and supplies. Sons of farmers found employment in the Middle Haddam yards and many East Hampton farmers provided timber for ship construction. Through this trade and small-scale manufacturing, East Hampton men had a firsthand familiarity with the marketplace that would have been foreign to a more remote agricultural community.

Early Industry: Setting the Tone

Lumbering operations required sawmills which tended to be established early in every New England town. Timbering often preceded agricultural development as a first step in clearing land. Lumber was also a cash crop and East Hampton's virgin forests attracted the attention of Middletown entrepreneurs ten years before East Hampton was settled.

East Hampton's first sawmill, built between 1729 and 1737, stood on Pocotopaug Stream. In 1740 a gristmill was built which suggests that there was an agricultural community sufficiently well established to supply it with corn or wheat. There were several other small-scale industries set up toward the end of the eighteenth century. Cider production required little capital investment and a

Top: The water tower and old buildings near what was the Siebert's Opera House in 1996. Courtesy Bernadette S. Prue

Bottom: Musicals and plays were a popular source of entertainment, such as this show at Siebert's Opera House in the 1930s. Courtesy Chatham Historical Society

number of farmers operated stills on their property. A tannery was built in the late 1780s. Shoemaking, a cottage industry that was quite widespread in East Hampton by the mid-nineteenth century, probably had its roots in this early enterprise.

The most significant early industry in East Hampton was the iron forge. In 1732 iron was discovered in Salisbury, Connecticut. Consequently, a number of forges were established in Litchfield County, in the vicinity of this mine. East Hampton's forge was exceptional in this respect. Established to refine Salisbury

Right: A 1996 view of the church. Courtesy Bernadette S. Prue

Below: The East Hampton Congregational Church was destroyed by fire in November of 1941. The fire started while paint was being stripped off the church. Courtesy Chatham Historical Society

iron little more than a decade after the ore's discovery, it was one of few Connecticut forges not located near the iron source. Built in 1744, the forge stood on the southern shore of Lake Pocotopaug at the mouth of the Pocotopaug Stream. It had at least one, and possibly two, waterwheels to convert the flow issuing from the lake into mechanical power.

In addition to introducing technology and outside investment into East Hampton, iron production involved local men in what must have been a fairly complex marketing network. The forge was started by outside capital and later drew in capital and skill from different parts of the state. Most significantly the forge provided a laboratory where generations of East Hampton men could observe firsthand the process of metal making. This familiarity was important in the eventual development of the bell industry.

In the nineteenth century, East Hampton's bell industry far surpassed the iron forge and the agriculturally related industries of the eighteenth century, and became the dominant force directing the town's development. In the 1820s several firms began manufacturing iron products, perpetuating and transforming the technology of the iron forge. Bellmaking grew up alongside this industry. Beginning on a small scale, bell founders gradually incorporated ironworking technology with the more subtle aspects of brass casting, and by 1850, monopolized bell production throughout the country.

Several local events prompted East Hampton's development in the early nineteenth century. Turnpike companies, funded by private investment, were established throughout Connecticut in the first decade of the nineteenth century. The Hebron Middle Haddam Turnpike, funded largely by Middle Haddam merchants, was established in 1802 to link Knowles Landing with the surrounding agricultural centers of East Hampton and

Mrs. Mary (Ray) Nichols packing toys made by the Gong Bell Company from 1940 to 1941. Gong Bell was established in 1866 under the partnership of H. H. Abbe, E. C. Barton, E. G. Cone, and A. H. Conklin. Mr. Barton was the originator of revolving chimes on bell toys that had wheels. The group photograph is a Gong Bell Company outing. Courtesy Chatham Historical Society

Hebron. Another turnpike linking Middletown and Colchester was established in 1808. The stage was set for industrialization. Economic and demographic changes forced farmers to consider new ways of investing their capital and energy. Local farmers demonstrated their resourcefulness by construction of the forge and mills and by involving themselves with Middle Haddam commerce and industry, as suppliers not merely of farm goods, but of labor and building supplies as well. Thus townsmen were prepared for the development of industry in the early nineteenth century.

Bellmaking: Resounding Changes

The fortuitous arrival of William Barton in 1807 determined the course of this industry. He set up shop and spent eighteen years in East Hampton practicing the bell trade. By 1819 East Hampton had six small bell furnaces. In the 1820s and 1830s, the forge and a number of sawmills along the stream were converted for the manufacture of iron products. Those who first ventured into manufacturing did not abandon farming immediately. Some set up shops on their farms so they could pursue both enterprises at once. But even for those involved in business partnerships, manufacturing life apparently proceeded at a fairly leisurely pace until around 1840.

While the manufacture of iron goods was significant in East Hampton's early industrial development, it was by its bell industry that East Hampton made its mark in the nineteenth century. By contributing the specialized technology required for bellmaking, William Barton enabled townsmen to compete successfully with other manufacturing centers, for East Hampton's sleighbells were not easily rivaled.

In 1837 Chauncey and Abner Bevin bought a plant on Pocotopaug Stream. The following year they admitted their younger brother Philo into the enterprise and took the name of Bevin Brothers Bell Company. In the following decade four other bell firms joined the Bevin Brothers on Pocotopaug Stream. The men who industrialized East Hampton also shaped much of the town's architecture. Architectural trends tended to parallel developments in the bell industry. The first houses built by bellmakers display Federal detailing which is somewhat unusual for so

late a date. But the bell industry got underway just prior to the widespread acceptance of the Greek Revival style, which is widespread among East Hampton houses dating from the mid-nineteenth century, demonstrating that this was a period of vitality in the village.

Competition prompted bell companies to diversify their lines. The Bevins began by producing sleighbells mounted on leather straps for attachment to a horse's harness. Later the Bevins and others began chime production. Firms also produced toy bells, call bells, tea bells and fancy tea bells, school bells, cowbells,

The Hiram Veazey House, located on West High Street, was erected in 1851 and enlarged on the east side in 1862. Hiram was the son of Eleazer Veazey. In 1842, he established a bell company, and was later joined by Alfred White under the name of Veazey and White. In 1882 it became Starr Brother's Bell Company and later Nesci Enterprises, Inc. Hiram's widow left the house to her nephew, William H. Bevin, who was also active in bell manufacturing. Courtesy Chatham Historical Society

Right: Center School circa 1869. Courtesy Middlesex County Historical Society

Below: The Niles House on Niles Street was originally constructed in 1852 by Stuart Parmelee. He was the partner of Dan B. Blies and Alexander Niles, forming Niles, Parmelee and Company. In 1863 Alexander Niles acquired full title, selling to Clark in the early 1900s. Courtesy Chatham Historical Society

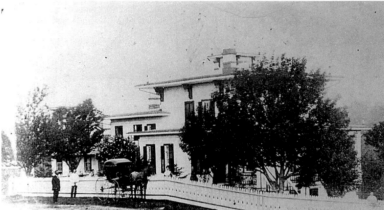

Right: This June 14, 1898, photograph shows John Howard Payne's home. Notes with the photograph indicate: "Monument in Tunis bears the inscription: In memory of John Howard Payne, author of 'Home Sweet Home'. Born June 9, 1791, died April 9, 1852. Erected AD 1855. Died at the American Consulate in Tunis, aged 60 years & 10 months. On Jan. 5, 1883, his remains were disinterred and taken to Washington where they were buried June 9, 1883 in Oak Hill Cemetery." Courtesy Middlesex County Historical Society

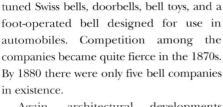

tuned Swiss bells, doorbells, bell toys, and a foot-operated bell designed for use in automobiles. Competition among the companies became quite fierce in the 1870s. By 1880 there were only five bell companies in existence.

Again, architectural developments reflected industrial changes. The houses built in downtown East Hampton between 1850 and 1860 were predominantly Greek Revival in style. During the period of accelerated competition between the bellmaking firms (1860–1880), East Hampton's most impressive Victorian houses were built by the owners of these companies. With these more imposing, almost ostentatious houses, these men seemed to be asserting their status in the community.

While East Hampton continued to develop in the later nineteenth century, the nature of town industries changed. Several new factories emerged in the 1880s and 1890s, each with different specializations so competition among local firms was reduced. A new development that altered town life was the railroad. While railroads often proved a great boon to industrial development, East Hampton's railroad arrived too late to bolster many of the already established firms.

The greatest benefit East Hampton derived from the railroad was the

Left: The Captain David Clark House was known as the "Inn." Built in 1737 by Alfonso Voisin, it was later owned by Captain Clark and was subsequently given to his great-grandson Chauncey W. Watrous. The house burned in 1900. Courtesy Chatham Historical Society

Below: The D. W. Watrous Manufacturing Company was established in 1857, manufacturing sleigh, hand, and other bells. D. W. Watrous is pictured standing on the stairs. Courtesy Chatham Historical Society

The Rapallo Viaduct was
built in 1912 for the Air Line
Railroad from Middletown.
It was sixty feet high by sixteen
hundred feet long and was
located two miles east of the
center of town. East Hampton
contributed $112,000 towards
the construction costs. Postcard
courtesy Middlesex County
Historical Society. Photographs
courtesy Chatham Historical
Society

Lakeview House was the first hotel on Lake Pocotopaug, looking from Sears Park. It was constructed about 1885 and was destroyed by fire in 1966. Courtesy Chatham Historical Society

Shown on this postcard is Edgemere Inn on Lake Pocotopaug, mailed August 22, 1930. Courtesy Middlesex County Historical Society

This French Second Empire house on Barton Hill Road was built by Philo Bevin, the youngest of four Bevin brothers, in 1872. It stayed in the Bevin family until the 1960s. Courtesy Bernadette S. Prue

Above: The N. N. Hill Brass Company was founded in 1889 and closed in the late 1950s. It manufactured bells and toys. The second photograph shows the enlarged building. Courtesy Chatham Historical Society

Right: Staff at Summer Camp Wopowog in 1940. Tourists from New York would come to East Hampton via train to attend. Courtesy Chatham Historical Society

development of the tourist industry. In the late nineteenth and early twentieth century the town became a summer resort catering to visitors who arrived by rail from New York. Lake Pocotopaug was the major attraction and a number of hotels and casinos sprang up along its shores. The railroad also fostered a new spurt of industrial growth, evidenced by the emergence of three large companies in the late nineteenth century to manufacture, sell and deal in cotton thread, silk, and linen fabric, manufacture xylophones and sleigh bells and produce bells by stamping them from sheet metal rather than casting. Norman N. Hill's stamping innovation was adopted by other companies as well, enabling them to remain competitive.

The railroad and Hill's ingenuity helped East Hampton keep pace with the world around it and brought the town's bell industry into the twentieth century. The Bevin Brothers Company is the only bell firm remaining in operation today, but the houses and factories built by the town's enterprising manufacturers serve as reminders of the history of this industry.

The Summit Thread Company was established in 1880, manufacturing a complete line of cotton thread and ready-wound bobbins for sewing machines. The company had offices in Boston, New York, Syracuse, Philadelphia, Baltimore, Cleveland, Cincinnati, St. Louis, and Dallas, discontining operations in the 1940s. Courtesy Chatham Historical Society

Above: Business Men's Baseball Team, parade and game on June 14, 1900. The teams were from the south and north ends of town. Courtesy Chatham Historical Society

Right: The 1916 Carnival of Fashion ladies pose in front of the Essie "Estelle" and Dora Dickson home on Miller Hill. Shown from left to right are: Florence Day, Marie Forand, Ethel Siebert, Lena Emerson, Netti Stevens, Essie Dickson, Dora Dickson, Beulah Brock (Middletown), Cornelia Watrous, Sophie Starr, Gloria Flynn, Annie Purple, Ada Sharpe (Middletown), Ruby Dickinson, Helen Sexton, Mildred Hall, Phyllis White, Lillian Russell, Cecelia Reardon, Irene Markham, and Miriam Burn. Courtesy Chatham Historical Society

These photographs of the 1938 Flood show:

Above: The Main Street Bakery, later Belltown Cleaners;

Top left: Summit Thread Company;

Middle left: Water rushing down a roadside. Courtesy Chatham Historical Society

Left: Looking South   on Main Street—Steve's Auto Sales on left, Seibert's Opera House in center, James Restaurant and Soda Shop to the side of the Opera House.

Right: The 1939 County League Champion Baseball Team. In the front row from left to right are: Raymond Cook and Kilbourne Gates. In the middle row are: James Costello, Richard Ferrari, Harold Bransfield, Adolph Frontel, Paul Bransfield, Gerald Wall, Frank Seckla, and Vincent Nelson. In the back row are: Charles Barber, Edward Bransfield, Gabriel Frontel, Leroy Bissell, Donald Mack, Thomas Wall, and Alfred Royce. Courtesy Chatham Historical Society

Above: The 1932 snowfall was severe. Center School is shown in the left photograph. Main Street looking north, with the railroad trestle in the background, is on the right. Courtesy Chatham Historical Society

Bottom: An early fire truck. Courtesy Chatham Historical Society

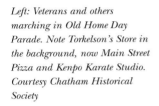

Left: Veterans and others marching in Old Home Day Parade. Note Torkelson's Store in the background, now Main Street Pizza and Kenpo Karate Studio. Courtesy Chatham Historical Society

Below: World War II veterans "Welcome Home Day" was photographed in 1946 on the hill behind the Post Office. Courtesy Chatham Historical Society

A tornado struck East Hampton on August 21, 1951, doing over $100,000 damage. Shown are two views of the East Hampton Congregational Church, Starr Brothers (the roof was blown off), and the intersection of Main Street and Barton Hill. Courtesy Chatham Historical Society

Left: Red Pepper Burns campaign car, from the eleventh Old Home Day Parade, goes by the Lutheran Church. Old Home Day was also referred to as the "East Hampton Belltown Carnival." Courtesy Chatham Historical Society

Below: Shown is St. Patrick's Catholic Church on Main Street in 1996. Courtesy Bernadette S. Prue

4
Haddam

Haddam's historic streetscapes invite nostalgic reflection on a time when the wilderness of Connecticut had only recently been tamed by the Puritan settlers. Indeed, the many sturdy, eighteenth-century houses in the town stand in mute testimony to this era. But Haddam was more than an isolated Colonial farm village. The original communal settlement of subsistence farmers was soon to disintegrate; even in

This old postcard of the Cotton Mill Dam and Flume represents the dozens of mills that flourished in the area from early in the nineteenth century through part of the twentieth. By the time such men as Hezekiah Scovil and Giles Brainerd began manufacturing their wares, there were five gristmills, nine sawmills, seven tanneries, two cider mills, and a gin distillery. Courtesy Haddam Historical Society

Above: Probably made in the early nineteenth century, this drawing shows the Haddam Court House in the center, with the Congregational Church behind. The East Haddam Landing near the Salmon River can be seen in the distance. Courtesy Jim Sarbaugh

Right: David Brainerd was an indentured servant when he came to Haddam as one of the first settlers. He became one of the town's most prominent citizens, and was a commissioner of the General Court in Hartford, justice of the peace, constable, surveyor, assessor, and deacon of the church. Courtesy Jim Sarbaugh

this early period there was not enough land to support the rapidly growing population. After the Revolution Haddam developed a thriving mercantile economy. Landless sons made careers in trading, shipbuilding, and small-scale industry; the Puritan became a Yankee. A "modern" man emerged—one who saw beyond the family farm to the seemingly limitless opportunities afforded by the Connecticut River and the water power of Haddam's streams.

Each part of Haddam possesses a distinctive architectural character which reflects the historical experience and values of its inhabitants. Only the "outlands" still truly reflect the rural agricultural life that sustained Haddam's people in the eighteenth century. Many of the older homes in the town center were replaced after the Revolution. These newer houses, as well as several commercial and institutional buildings, reflect the vitality of Haddam's role as a half-shire town. These Federal-period buildings were fashionable but not overly ostentatious displays of wealth. To the east across the Connecticut River is Haddam Neck. Its architecture expresses its isolation and unique relationship with the parent town. In the southern part of town, nineteenth-century mariners sailed from the riverport of Tylerville, many in ships built here on the bank of the river, but returned to Tylerville and neighboring Shailerville to their homes–dwellings that expressed the reluctance of these conservative communities to give up the traditional values of the eighteenth century. In Higganum, in the northern part of town, the bustling shipyards, warehouses, and wharves at the Landing are all gone; only a small cluster of houses remains. Simple cottages standing next to more formal houses tell the story of a prosperous riverport that flourished here for almost one hundred years. The development of industry on Higganum's waterways in the later nineteenth century produced a more sophisticated and diverse architecture: the majestic mansions of the factory owners, the simpler dwellings of the foremen or managers, and the modest residences of the workers—all coexisting with the earlier eighteenth-century houses. Here too, many factories remain as a reminder of the ingenuity, courage, and hard work that brought Higganum fully into the modern industrial world and made it a vital economic center of the town.

Haddam is a historical microcosm, influenced by the great movements of Colonial settlement, the Revolution, the birth of a new country, and the economic growth and eventual decline of the industrial revolution in New England; its architecture reflects the impact of historical change and the attitudes and values of those who lived through these periods.

The Colonial Experience

The Colonial experience in Haddam is almost inaccessible to the modern historian. Beyond the nostalgic recollections of a series of Haddam historians who saw the town's past as an arcadian idyll, the reality of the period from settlement to the Revolution is almost lost in the gloss of time. Land and probate records reveal the movement of property among the living and between the living and the dead; vital records and genealogies trace the growth and scattering of Haddam families. But early church records provide only glimpses into the institutional life of the community, and few firsthand accounts remain to tell us of the everyday life of the townspeople. By contrast, contention with neighboring towns or internal religious and political conflict is well documented in town and colony records, so much that it tends to bias our view of the town's life. We must place what little we know of Haddam's history in the context of early Connecticut history, or compare it to the

This simple clapboard schoolhouse served the children of Shailerville well in the early twentieth century. It was moved from Saybrook Road to Old Turnpike Road in 1921 because of a new hazard—the automobile. "It's considered dangerous," wrote teacher Elizabeth Hutchinson Bedini, "because a car might happen along, and most of the children would have to cross that road." The building is now a private home. Courtesy Haddam Historical Society

Below: The "Old Burial Yard of Thirty Mile Island" is the earliest cemetery in Haddam. It is on a knoll overlooking Haddam Meadows State Park. Courtesy Haddam Historical Society

115

The settlers of the towns in the Massachusetts Bay Colony, in effect employees of the Massachusetts Bay Company, covenanted together to form a community. The idea of a covenant with God would be the informing metaphor and governing principle for new towns for at least a hundred years, but their economic relationship more closely resembled a joint stock company. Each man's share in the company was the homelot he purchased when a new town was laid out. Skilled craftsmen were valued in establishing a new town, and frequently would-be settlers such as housewrights, blacksmiths, and millers were given land in a new town as their shares in a company to encourage them to emigrate. Although the settlers in each town lived in small nucleated settlements after the pattern of the English manorial village, with land set aside for the meetinghouse and the cow commons, they fully expected that the remaining commonly owned land would be divided up among them according to the value of their investment.

Thirty Mile Island Plantation

In 1662 the first Englishmen arrived to settle Thirty Mile Island Plantation, coming downriver to "plant" the town in the year the royal charter was issued to the Connecticut Colony by Charles II. The plantation was named for the large island in the Connecticut River (now Haddam Island) believed at that time to be thirty miles from Long Island Sound. The land had been purchased for the settlers by Matthew Wyllys and John Allyn, agents for the colony. Scrupulous in their dealings with the Indians, these men had already "paid" for the land with thirty coats estimated to have been worth about $100. Although the Indians set aside a buffer zone of forty acres at Cove Meadow in Chester, and reserved the right to Haddam Island as well as their right to hunt and fish

history of nearby towns to reach an understanding of the people and the times. Only then do we find that the community's Colonial experience was neither the idyllic existence imagined by her proud descendants nor the dispute-ridden struggle that the public records would suggest. Haddam, in fact, was settled by men and women of good will who were sent to Thirty Mile Island Plantation to build a town. As over 320 years of existence attest, they succeeded very well.

where they pleased, by the early 1700s the Indian population had practically disappeared except for small groups in East Haddam, on Haddam Island, and at a hollow on Haddam Neck (off today's Injun Hollow Road).

Like the Mattabeseck Plantation (now Middletown), Thirty Mile Island Plantation encompassed land on both sides of the "Grate River" as it was called in this period. The areas of settlement were quite small: two locations on high ground above the west bank of the river. The Town Plot, the larger of the two settlements, was laid out along the southern end of the present Walkley Hill Road to about the site of the old graveyard. The Lower Plantation was south of Mill Creek, in the area known today as Shailerville, and was concentrated near the creek on today's Park and Old Turnpike Roads. Land was set aside in the Town Plot for the meetinghouse and the minister's homelot, perhaps less as an expression of piety than to fulfill a requirement of the General Court.

The township bounds, as recorded in the original deed, encompassed all the remaining unsettled land on both sides of the Connecticut River between Middletown and Saybrook, an area of 104.3 square miles. Because the plantation was located well below the alluvial floodplain of the river, Connecticut's prime crop-growing belt, most of the land was of poor quality, only suitable for growing grain or for haying and pasturage. Only 5 percent was prime growing land. The better land was concentrated in the area of the first settlements, and in the natural meadows along the riverbank; the marginal land was located in the valleys of the major streams. The thin soil of the upland was full of boulders, as miles of old stone walls in Haddam attest.

The Connecticut River was a major resource, a principal transportation artery for almost two hundred years. At several "landings" on the west side of the river, shipyards and small trading ports were established by the middle of the

eighteenth century. From the beginning, fish were seined from the river every spring, adding to the food supply. On the east side the Salmon River is joined on its journey to the Connecticut River by Pine Brook as it cuts across the northern edge of Haddam Neck. These smaller streams became valuable as a source of water power.

Usually, at least fifty heads of household were needed to support the church in a new town. Each would be taxed by the town in goods, services, or cash to pay the minister's rate and to build the meetinghouse and parsonage. The Haddam settlement contained less than

The Grand Army of the Republic was the predecessor of modern-day veteran's groups. These Civil War Veterans were taking part in ceremonies marking Decoration Day 1905, a holiday that began with the end of the Civil War and would become known as Memorial Day after World War I. Only a few are identified: fourth from left: Daniel Priest, seventh: Clayton Hartman, and tenth: George Russell. Courtesy Haddam Historical Society

Abraham Symons was a Narragansett Indian who settled in Haddam. This stone was erected in the Higganum Cemetery on Pokorny Road in Symon's memory in 1925 by the students of Dartmouth College. Dartmouth had a long-standing tradition of allowing Native Americans to attend the school free of charge. Courtesy Haddam Historical Society

The horse and buggy was an important method of transportation. Courtesy Haddam Historical Society

half this number initially, but the number of original proprietors was close to the average for towns established before 1675.

Early efforts to build a meetinghouse were almost as unsuccessful as those made to attract and keep a minister. The town voted in 1670 to "bilde," with a committee to assign the work to each man "a cording to their proporsiones." The rate was set several times to pay for the house, but it was three years before the building was framed out, and it was not sheathed in clapboards or shingled for many years. Whether the first meetinghouse was ever completely finished is not recorded. The need for a larger meetinghouse occupied the town's attention by 1718; actual construction did not start until 1721. By this time Haddam had sixty-two heads of household and the town was sufficiently prosperous to support a church society.

Civil affairs also claimed the attention of the townspeople. Efforts were made to settle the ownership of the commonly owned land outside the original settlement areas. Most of the conflicts over boundary claims with neighboring towns were resolved by the early 1670s. The line with Middletown to the north was easily established, but settlement of the boundaries with Saybrook and Killingworth on the west side of the river and with Lyme on the east, were more complicated. It was not until 1671 that a committee of men from Saybrook and Haddam surveyed the dividing line and fixed the boundary.

A series of events made it quite clear that the King was reasserting his control and the colonies were now to become a major part of the British Empire. The colony was concerned about the legal status of her towns and took steps to legalize ownership of town lands. In 1668 Thirty Mile Island Plantation was officially designated a town and renamed Haddam (probably after Hadham, England) as part of this effort. Future events proved that these fears were justified: within a decade, land titles in New York and Massachusetts would be invalidated by Governor Andros, sent by the Crown to be the royal governor of New England.

The residents of Haddam began to spread out from the original settlement areas as soon as the land was divided. After the land between the two original town plots was settled, some families migrated farther to start new settlements. A few families moved north, making a settlement at "Hegamumpos" (Higganum) between 1685 and 1700. Haddam Neck was settled between 1710 and 1712. The majority of its settlers came from Haddam, although some were from Lyme and Chatham (now East Hampton and Portland).

A century of sustained population growth threatened to overturn the traditional way of life of the Colonial farmer. Haddam had approximately five hundred people in 1720 (sixty-two heads of household in 1719) and grew steadily. By the Revolution the population had increased to 1,726, thirteen of whom were listed as Negroes, probably slaves. Even if the town had remained its original size, the limited land resources would have been severely strained. But the vast acreage of the Thirty Mile Island Plantation was considerably reduced over the years. Land lost in the boundary settlements, and more importantly by the separation from East Haddam, had reduced the original tract by half. By 1773, with the loss of the Haddam Quarter to Durham, the town contained only 46.7 square miles, or about thirty thousand acres, the size it is today. The amount of land available for growing crops was so small that the population problem must have been acute when the third generation came of age. With only forty-five hundred acres of tillable land, Haddam could provide a bare subsistence living for only a hundred farming families. The town contained more than twice that many by the middle of the eighteenth century.

Land scarcity and over-population contributed to other social and economic problems in the New England colonies. There was a predictable spread of epidemic diseases beginning in the 1730s. Arranged marriages were delayed for lack of land or a dowry. Premarital conceptions increased dramatically, forcing many parents to give their permission for marriage. The price of land rose and contributed to the general inflation of the times, adding to a reduction in the standard of living. The steady stream of imported English goods that the colonists had come to expect was cut off by a war in the West Indies with the improbable name of "The War of Jenkin's Ear." Within a decade, a migration of settlers into the interior of the colonies would force England and France to battle over dominion over the North American continent in the French and Indian or "Seven Years' War."

The Revolutionary Experience

Haddam men, like all the "reluctant revolutionaries" of other New England towns, were prepared to fight to defend their homes or their families. Indeed from the beginning of the settlement the "traine band" and the militia companies were set up expressly for this purpose. In 1775, when dispatch riders brought the news from Massachusetts of the "shot heard 'round the world," Haddam responded to the Lexington Alarm with a troop of militia commanded by Colonel Tyler.

After it became apparent that the Revolution was turning into a protracted all-out war, there appeared not only the "reluctance [of men in Haddam] to leave their firesides . . . [for] service on distant fields," but also a general reluctance on the part of the towns to respond to any demands of the state government for more supplies or money. No longer able to obtain what was needed by persuasion, the state had to resort to coercion. Incentives and bonuses designed to encourage volunteer enlistments in the army were only partially successful, and had to be replaced with compulsory drafts.

Originally built for Edward and Cynthia (Selden) Munger in 1818, this house was sold to Reverend Marsh in 1821. It remained a Congregationalist parsonage until 1849. Courtesy Haddam Historical Society

The Comfort Cone House was built circa 1830 for Comfort (1795–1876), the son of Noadiah and Elizabeth (Clark) Cone. He married wealthy Ann Brooks, farmed for a living, and was Deacon of the Congregational Church from 1841 to 1844. His estate was purchased by Martha Davis, wife of Clinton B. Davis of the Higganum Manufacturing Company. The house began as a typical federal design, but has been added to several times; it currently has three staircases, four fireplaces and numerous rooms. In its racier days in the early twentieth century, it was widely known in the area as a bordello. It has now been renovated and stands as a beautiful example of its era on Walkley Hill Road. Courtesy Jody and Arthur Blake

With the constant movement in and out of the army, fewer men were available to bring in the harvest. Not only did labor shortages cause a decline in agricultural production; the war also brought increased demands for what food and animal fodder was produced. Town taxes in Haddam were paid in provisions, with beef, pork, and wheat flour accepted at fixed rates. That same year, volunteers for the army were promised a special bonus. In addition to their wages and a bounty for enlisting, the town offered a bonus of thirty-five shillings per month, to be paid in wheat. Given the devalued state of the currency, wheat was worth more than money.

Although Haddam experienced a building boom after the Revolution, housing conditions varied and reflected the growing disparity between economic classes. Families involved in trade or industry built larger, more formal houses for their sons, but many married sons from poorer families could no longer count on starting out their married lives in homes of their own. By the early decades of the nineteenth century, several generations of the same family often shared the same house. Even the types of houses that were built suggest that the community as a whole was only moderately prosperous. Almost as many of the smaller Cape-style houses were built after the Revolution as were constructed during the Colonial period; the larger houses were quite

traditional, with limited architectural detail.

The first true architectural style to become popular in Haddam was the Federal style. In some instances, older Colonials were updated with Federal-style detailing, inside and out, but to the casual observer, the houses built after 1790 still have a Colonial appearance, primarily because practically every house retained the center-chimney stack.

The Georgian style eliminated the massive central chimney and had a center-hall plan with smaller interior chimneys equally spaced out towards the end walls. This style is quite rare in Haddam, with only two examples still existing. The center-hall-plan house was more than a structural change or simply a question of taste. Rather, it was a response to changing ideas about the family and the new importance of the individual. The communal living pattern of the Colonial period was discarded in favor of a greater degree of privacy for members of the family.

In Haddam, however, domestic architecture rarely reflected the new ideas about family and individuals. The central-chimney house continued to be built right through the Federal period, apparently quite deliberately. The essentially conservative nature of Haddam is best illustrated by the surviving Federal-period architecture in Shailerville, where

eighteenth-century family and building traditions persisted until the middle of the nineteenth century. After 1830 the Federal style was gradually transformed into the typical Greek revival form, the first truly American style.

Haddam, the Half-Shire Town

The formation of Middlesex County by an act of the legislature in 1785 had a great impact on the town of Haddam. Created from portions of Hartford and New London Counties, Middlesex County originally consisted of six towns: Middletown, Chatham (East Hampton and Portland), Haddam, East Haddam (all originally part of Hartford County); and Saybrook and Killingworth (from New London County). In 1799 these six were joined by Durham, which broke away from New Haven County. Because of their central location in the county, Middletown and Haddam were chosen to be "half-shire towns"—that is, to share the county seat. The effect of this appointment and the resulting prosperity is clearly reflected even today in the appearance of the town center. The first county courthouse and jail, built in 1786, are no longer standing, but over half of the other surviving historic buildings in the center were constructed during Haddam's heyday as a half-shire town (1785–1840).

An additional stimulus to development was the Middlesex Turnpike, which opened in 1802 and ran right through the middle of Haddam. This thirty-two-mile stretch of road from Wethersfield to Saybrook both encouraged the town's growth as a commercial and institutional center and made it more accessible to the outside world. Merchants, craftsmen, innkeepers, and professionals clustered along the new turnpike near the courthouse and jail. Although Haddam's modern commercial focus had shifted to

The Sheriff's Shack. During the Depression, Burt G. Thompson and his family hosted baseball games and enormously popular dinners, complete with china and silver, on the spacious verandah of this building, built for that purpose. It was located near what is now the boat launch at Haddam Meadows State Park. Courtesy Haddam Historical Society

Higganum and Tylerville at the crossroads of major highways, in the early nineteenth century Haddam Center was the focal point for the development of the town.

By the end of the eighteenth century, Haddam was no longer a country village but was a regional center with a major attraction to visitors, the county court. Attendance at court trials was even more of a spectator sport in the nineteenth century than it is today, and curiosity-seekers flocked to town when court was in session. If court cases lasted more than a day, there were a number of places to stay overnight. At least six of the thirty-three houses built in Haddam Center at this time also served as taverns, with accommodations for overnight guests.

Predictably, the more visible wealth of the mercantile economy coupled with an increase in the number of transients brought an increase in the crime rate, especially in crimes of violence against persons and property. The first jail, a wooden building which was built across from the present jail, sometimes housed genuine criminals, but served mainly as a debtors' prison. The present jail was built in 1845: a masonry complex which contained the jailkeeper's stone "mansion," with cells and a workhouse attached on the west wall. The prison walls were solid granite, two feet thick, with special attention paid to security precautions.

Nehemiah and John Brainerd opened a granite quarry south of the center in 1794. This not only provided jobs for as many as a hundred men at a time in its successful years, but also affected the appearance of the center's streetscape by providing materials for the construction of several fine-quality stone buildings. Built in 1838 by Nehemiah and John Brainerd, the Brainerd Academy sits above the town on Isinglass Hill. Easily the most impressive of all the granite buildings, it was built in the Greek Revival style, and was originally three stories tall. The roof was lowered and the cupola removed in 1930.

Shipping played a part in the development of Haddam Center from 1790 until 1807, when the Great Embargo cut back the amount of trade to area ports.

A wharf and landing area, often called Proprietors' Wharf in the land records, was located along the bank of the Connecticut River in Haddam Center. Several stores located at the landing received goods from ships brought from nearby ports and the West Indies.

The commercial heyday of Haddam Center was short-lived. Its decline was caused partly by the War of 1812, which restricted the amount of goods reaching inland ports throughout New England. Haddam Landing appears never to have fully recovered from setbacks suffered during this era. Haddam's position as a half-shire town was also slowly deteriorating in the 1820s, as Middletown strengthened its dominance in the state. By 1825 dissatisfaction with the split county seat had begun to be mentioned in newspaper articles. The modest facilities of the Haddam courthouse were also a source of contention, although the *New Haven Journal* probably exaggerated when it referred to the building in 1825 as being "Inferior to hundreds of barns in the County of Middlesex." Evidently Haddam

Brainerd Academy trained young men in the classics, with students coming from as far away as Ceylon. It closed in 1890 and the building was given to the town in 1929. The third story and bell tower were removed in 1930. Courtesy Haddam Historical Society

was having difficulties meeting the financial demands of being a county seat. Yet in 1829, when the people of Middletown expressed a desire to locate the seat exclusively in Middletown, "Haddam sturdily resisted this suggestion" and subsequently built a new stone courthouse in the town center. The two towns continued to share the county seat until the 1880s, when renewed pressure from Middletown finally resulted in the moving of the county court to the larger city. After the move the Haddam courthouse became the town hall, and continued as such until the building burned in 1929.

As the century progressed, the importance of the Middlesex Turnpike declined. The increased steamboat traffic on the Connecticut River in mid-century attracted travelers who had formerly passed through Haddam Center. The decline in the number of turnpike users was further compounded by the opening of the Connecticut Valley Railroad in 1871. Running along the river's edge from Old Saybrook to Hartford, the railroad provided a faster and more scenic route for travelers who had once made their way through the heart of Haddam on the turnpike.

The County Orphanage, built in 1887, was the last building constructed in response to Haddam's responsibilities as half-shire town. Although Haddam had relinquished its role as the county seat, the

orphanage operated for a countywide area until 1955. The last historic institutional building to be erected in Haddam Center was the Brainerd Memorial Library. Perhaps the most distinguished architectural contribution to the center's historic streetscape, it was donated to the town in 1908 by members of two leading families.

Higganum, the Shipping and Industrial Center

Water power attracted the first settlers to Higganum. The area to the north and west of the original plantation settlement

Top: The view from Isinglass Hill, showing Haddam Center and the courthouse that was destroyed in 1929. Courtesy Haddam Historical Society

Bottom: Local quarries in the late eighteenth and early nineteenth centuries produced significant quantities of granite and sandstone. The Shaler family operated one quarry well into the nineteenth century, shipping from Arnold's Landing. Courtesy Haddam Historical Society

Above: The death of a little girl, despite efforts by Mrs. E. W. N. Starr to adopt her, led to the establishment of the Middlesex County Orphan's Home in 1877. Initially supported and run by wealthy women, state support began in 1883. It is now the University of Connecticut Agricultural Extension Center. Courtesy Middlesex County Historical Society

Right: The Higganum Station of the New York, New Haven & Hartford Railroad, at the foot of Landing Road, was used heavily by shoppers and high school students who had to travel to Middletown until regional high schools opened in the 1930s. Courtesy Haddam Historical Society

contained some of the best "water privileges," as water rights on the streams were called in this part of the Connecticut Valley. A gristmill, already operating by 1678, was soon followed by several mills in the eighteenth century. By the nineteenth century, most of the twenty-seven mills and "manufactories" in Haddam were located in Higganum. The water privileges along these streams were valuable property that was handed down from one generation to the next for several hundred years. Water-powered mills of various kinds continued to operate until the twentieth century.

Higganum Landing

A natural harbor at Higganum Cove was well suited for the development of a riverport, which came to be known as Higganum Landing. A store was opened at the Landing in 1752. After the construction of the first ship in 1754 and the opening of the ferry between Haddam Neck and Higganum in 1763 by Jabez Brainerd, Higganum's riverport grew steadily.

Independence from England did not immediately bring about a resumption of foreign trade. It was not long, however, before the skilled mariners and shipbuilders in Haddam who had made the Revolution their training ground established themselves in the maritime and shipping trade. After 1789, when West Indies ports were opened to neutral carriers, fortunes could be made, especially while the war between England and France continued. Shipbuilding in Haddam flourished to meet the demand.

The entire town of Haddam usually had five or six vessels in the coastal trade and two or three trading with the West Indies. Local products, shipped directly from

Brainerd Memorial Library, a combination Beaux Arts and Colonial Revival building, is an architectural gem. It was primarily funded by a gift from Cyprian Strong Brainerd, providing the Haddam Library Association with a permanent home. Courtesy Susan M. Freimuth

J. E. Cronin & Co. Groceries and Provisions. Courtesy Middlesex County Historical Society

Higganum Landing, most likely were limited to cattle, hogs, timber, and later, stone. These exports were traded for necessary goods not available locally, such as molasses and salt, and for bills of exchange for English luxury goods. Timber, which the town had in abundance, was a valuable commodity for trade, for both building and cordwood.

Although the Non-Intercourse Act, signed into law in March of 1809, allowed American merchants to trade with any port not under British or French control, the business of building ships never returned to its former production level at Higganum. Only one ship was constructed in 1809 and one in 1810, indicating the unwillingness of local merchants to risk their capital and goods. Commerce had virtually ceased by the War of 1812. The Child yard built two "gunboats" for the government during the war, and continued to prosper until the 1850s, but by 1830 the rest of the Connecticut shipbuilding industry was generally in a sharp decline, and the focus of maritime activities had shifted to major East Coast ports. Not only were the heavily wooded forests of the Connecticut River valley depleted, but most of the deep-draft ships in demand in this period were too large to be built in shipyards on inland rivers.

The Industries

As shipbuilding declined, some resourceful Yankees in Higganum were already involved in manufacturing, building their mills at the site of earlier grist- and sawmills. Few of these early factories were successful, but there were some exceptions. Several improved and efficient grist- and sawmills continued to run for most of the nineteenth century.

The oldest commercial establishment in continuous use in the area, the Higganum Feed Store was built circa 1880 by Buckley E. Johnson. Felix Petrofsky, owner from 1924 to 1945, is shown in front of the store. Brainard Hall, shown circa 1891, had many uses. The ground floor, which was the Post Office and McAvay Drug Store, is now the Country Market. The upper floor, now the Grange Hall, was used for everything from movies to high school graduations. Courtesy Haddam Historical Society

It was not until 1844 and the formation of the D.&H. Scovil Hoe Company that Higganum really began to take its place in the industrial revolution. Daniel and Hezekiah were the sons of Hezekiah Scovil, Sr. (1788–1849), who had learned the blacksmith trade from his uncle David Spencer. Hezekiah manufactured hammers and other agricultural tools at a site near his residence on Candlewood Hill Road. Later he was apprenticed to Eli Whitney in New Haven to learn the art of welding gun barrels. About 1810 he converted his mill to a gun barrel factory and supplied the government under contract in the War of 1812. Both Daniel and Hezekiah were trained by their father in the metalworking trades.

Separation

Higganum had been part of Haddam for almost two hundred years, but by the mid-eighteenth century the family and religious ties that had held the two communities together were considerably weakened. Higganum residents had agitated for their own church society as early as 1738. Their petition to the General Court was denied. In the 1760s the

location of a new church building to serve both communities became a source of contention. When it became apparent that there was little chance of a decision favorable to Higganum, the residents renewed their petition to the General Court for their own society but were again denied. It was only a matter of time, however, before these efforts would be renewed and would succeed. The final split in 1844 with the Haddam Church, the First Society, was not an amicable separation.

In 1859 Higganum submitted a petition to the state legislature to become a

Opposite page: This photograph is believed to be of George S. Arnold. It shows the elaborate outfits available to the well-to-do.

Left: George S. Arnold in military uniform. Courtesy Haddam Historical Society

separate town. It is not clear why the petitioners were unsuccessful in their bid to have official recognition for a separation that existed in all but name. Their request was approved by a joint committee of the legislature, as well as by the Senate, but it was denied in the House and finally defeated. The record shows the depth of resentment and degree of animosity that existed between the two districts.

Victorian Architecture

The extraordinary variety of Victorian architecture was made possible because of machine-age improvements in building technology. The underpinnings of the house, the frame, and the nails that held the frame together were mass-produced. The newer wire nails were very inexpensive, quite a change from the early days when the town had to sell land to have the money to buy nails from the blacksmith to build the parsonage. Once they were no longer limited to the simple box-like forms that could be framed with posts and beams, designers and builders could indulge in the complex floor plans and unusual shapes that characterized the Victorian house.

No longer the seemingly classless society suggested by the architecture of the Colonial period, Higganum emerged in the nineteenth century as a clearly stratified society. The factory owner no longer lived near his business. He built his mansion on the hill overlooking the town, while his workers still lived amid the noise and pollution near the factory. In the "Middletown Tribune Souvenir Edition of 1896" engravings of the most elaborate, ostentatious houses built in Higganum at this time are reproduced. They include the grand and gaudy Thomas J. Clark House on Saybrook Road, and the elegant and imposing brick Queen Anne-style mansion built by Hezekiah Scovil.

Above: Miner Comstock Hazen, a physician, was one of Haddam's most prominent late nineteenth-century citizens. He and his wife Lemira were parents of Edward, a noted philanthropist. Natives of Agawam, Massachusetts, Dr. and Mrs. Hazen came to Haddam in 1860. Nine years later, they built an imposing Greek Revival house on Walkley Hill Road. Edward was state representative (1917–1919) and state senator (1919–1921) from Haddam. In 1925 he formed the Hazen Foundation, which supported, among others, Middlesex Hospital and the Northern Middlesex YMCA, whose summer camp is named for the family. Courtesy Haddam Historical Society

Top and bottom left: Harley Davis Peck of Candlewood Hill Road stands by a team of oxen in this undated photograph. Oxen were used into the early 1900s for plowing, as well as ice-cutting on local ponds and the Connecticut River. Courtesy Haddam Historical Society

Right: Postcard of the main road in Haddam, now called Saybrook Road (Route 154). Courtesy Susan M. Freimuth

Bottom right: The Leatherman has long ties in local folklore. Courtesy Haddam Historical Society

130

Top: Parade ready—on the left is Jarvis Ryan. The other gentleman is unidentified. Courtesy Haddam Historical Society

Bottom: Austin S. Clark went West after gold, but never made it to California. He returned to fish at his camp and to become a State Senator. Courtesy Haddam Historical Society

Right: Workmen pose in the fall of 1912. Courtesy Haddam Historical Society.

Below: The completed bridge was greeted with "a rush of autos," according to the Penny Press. *Courtesy Middlesex County Historical Society*

Right: Hezekiah Scovil, inventor of the planter's hoe, had this Queen Anne-style house erected on Maple Avenue in 1875. It was inherited by his nephew, Whitney S. Porter, in 1904. From 1947 to 1982 it was a Roman Catholic convent, finally reverting to a private home. Courtesy Haddam Historical Society

Above: Opened in 1913, the swing bridge over the Connecticut River between Goodspeed's Landing and Tylerville, was a marvel of its day. The Goodspeed Opera House is clearly visible, with the span under construction.

SHAD FISHING IN CONN RIVER
HADDAM, CONN.

Top: Bible Rock, across from
Seven Falls State Park, was a
popular tourist site at the turn
of the century. The granite slabs
were named for their resemblance
to a partly open bible. Courtesy
Haddam Historical Society

Middle and bottom: Irving and
Alice Bailey of Bridge Road in
Tylerville, repair shad nets.
In 1818 there were seventeen
separate places in Haddam and
Higganum where the prized fish
were caught. Spencer's Shad
Shack on Route 154, open only
for a few weeks each spring when
the shad are running, used to
supply Fulton Fish Market. The
photograph of nets is courtesy
Haddam Historical Society
and the photograph of fishing
is courtesy Middlesex County
Historical Society

5
Middlefield

From its beginnings in the early eighteenth century, Middlefield has been a village of "Outlivers," a satellite of Middletown. Unlike the "typical" New England village, Middlefield was never a neatly centered community; instead, it was made up of a widely scattered group of farms, whose inhabitants were not always interested in coming together as a religious and civic community. The first three settlers lived some distance apart, Benjamin Miller on his father's lot near the Durham line in the south, Samuel Allen, also on his father's property over three miles away near the northern border, and

Jackson Hill Road by the North Burying Ground. The 1737 deed for the burying ground carried the name of an early settler, John Brown. Courtesy Middlefield Historical Society

135

The Congregational Church in Middlefield. Courtesy Ray Hubbard

Samuel Wetmore near the center of town, probably on the Stow lot. Another early settler was John Brown. These men and their families were soon joined by others: the Coes came from Stratford, the Birdseys from Durham, and the Bartletts from Guilford, all to settle on land purchased from Middletown proprietors or their descendants.

Although these men came from different places in the colony, they were still a homogeneous group. They were all Englishmen, all Puritans, and quite probably all descendants of English farmers. Their similar social and religious backgrounds influenced the ways they built their houses, tilled the land, and worshipped, but they were apparently not enough to enable them to agree for very long on a single minister or even a common brand of Protestantism.

In 1743 the fledgling community petitioned the General Court to become a separate parish. Approval came the following year, along with the customary requirement that a meetinghouse be built within a certain period of time. Although by colony law all the village inhabitants had to support the parish church and its minister, the Congregational church was less of a force in Middlefield than elsewhere in Connecticut. Several forces worked against the formation of a strong

and influential church. The dispersed settlement pattern of Middlefield had an effect. More importantly, the Middlefield church was formed when Congregationalism itself was in turmoil. Controversies over admission to communion, over the authority of the clergy, and the "Great Awakening" all acted to diminish the respect accorded the church and its clergymen. The issue that most undermined the effectiveness of the village church, however, had to do with the persistence of the Middletown church as the center of civic and religious authority. In Middletown, as in other Connecticut towns, the church and the government were virtually one body: the town meeting was simply the congregation reconstituted for political purposes. For the men of Middlefield to participate in the government of the town they had to attend town meetings in Middletown. Election to town offices was predicated on such attendance, since townsmen would be unlikely to elect someone they didn't know, especially if he was an "outliver." Middlefield settlers maintained close civic and religious ties with Middletown for at least another seventy-five years after the establishment of the Middlefield parish. During this period, in fact, 30 percent of all those elected to office in Middletown actually came from Middlefield. Ultimately, secular concerns worked against the establishment of a true community in Middlefield and weakened the influence of the church.

Middlefield's first minister, Ebenezer Gould, was dismissed after some controversy by 1756, never to preach again. Nine years elapsed before another minister was appointed, and he died at an early age in 1770, to be succeeded by a fellow graduate of Yale College, who was himself dismissed in 1785. After this "the pulpit was vacant for twenty years—the old professors of religion died or removed, until the church was almost extinct." Church records indicate that worship did continue intermittently and informally, however. New Protestant sects emerged in this period, making inroads into pure old-style Congregationalism. Even when the church was re-established in 1808, the members were still a divided group, and still just as intolerant. The old meeting-house was still serviceable but they couldn't agree on its use, first building a new, shared meetinghouse, and later in the century establishing separate places of worship for the Congregationalists and the Methodists.

Building a Community

The town's first settler was "Governor" Benjamin Miller, the fourth son of Thomas Miller, a Middletown proprietor. Benjamin came of age in 1693, married his first wife, Mary Johnson, two years later and moved to Middlefield. They had eight children; Mary died as her son Ichabod was being born. Benjamin married Mercy Bassett the following year, and they had seven more children. The original tract of land that Benjamin inherited was only 157.5 acres, quite small compared to the size of other proprietors' lots in Middlefield. By the time of his death in 1747, however, Benjamin was the largest single property owner in the village and the Miller family owned over 20 percent of the land, an estimated 1,300 acres.

Although the house that Governor Benjamin Miller built near the corner of Cherry Hill Road and Miller Road no longer stands, houses built by the descendants who bore his name still exist. One, the David Miller House on Miller Road, is located near the home farm on the original tract "set" to his father in the

Here we see the Middlefield Federated Church. The inside was decorated with fancy wall painting and a notable chandelier with eight double-globe lamps. When the chandelier was removed, some of the globes were made into table lamps. This photograph of the congregation on the outside steps was taken in the 1930s. Courtesy Ray Hubbard

Queens of Middlefield's Apple Blossom Festivals: Misses Lois Fowler (1935), Edith Mousch (1936), Edith Link (1933), Doris Way (1938), Dorothea Schaub (1937), and Cecelia Garbognola (1934). The townspeople voted for the queen, paying a nickel per vote. Money from the festival, which was started by Rev. Applegath, supported the Middlefield Federated Church. Courtesy Ray Hubbard

Meek Road at Jackson Hill Road. Courtesy Middlefield Historical Society

seventeenth century. This brief biography of Benjamin Miller illustrates the importance of family, marriage, and land in Colonial culture. Through blood and marriage ties, families were knit together into a mutually supportive communal network. Within a few decades, reciprocal ties of kinship and obligation, both within and between generations, were reinforced, bringing together men and the land, binding them even more closely to each other and to the town.

The family regulated the behavior of its members and, since everyone was required to live in families, a certain patriarchal social order was achieved. Women deferred to men; men deferred to their "betters" and elders; children, even grown sons, deferred to their fathers. The elderly,

the sick, and the poor were also the responsibility of the family. When families could not manage incorrigible children, they were "bound out" to other families for discipline and training. In this male-dominated society, women were "civilly dead," dependent first on their fathers, then their husbands, and in old age, as widows, on their children.

Land in an eighteenth-century farming community was not only a source of food, but also the basis of the whole social and economic order, the reward to sons for obedience, the daughters' dowries, the resource that enabled families to take on the social responsibilities now carried on by the state. Ownership of land affected farming families in other ways that they perhaps only dimly understood. The rhythm of their lives was controlled by the cycle of the seasons.

Land, however, has no value unless it can be brought into production. The miles of stone walls that border Connecticut fields bear mute testimony to the intractability of the land. The rocky soil, however, was only one factor that made farming in the state difficult. New England's short growing season and limited labor supply were equally important. Colonial farming was labor intensive. Although some Middlefield farmers did own slaves, most depended upon their own families, especially their sons, for labor. This was particularly true at harvest time; a short harvest period required many hands.

This created a dilemma: sons were needed to bring land into production, but sons also had to be provided for, usually with shares of their father's land. As land grew scarcer, fathers became reluctant to part with it during their lifetime. One solution was to bind sons to the land by promises of inheritance which would not be fulfilled until their father died. This at least kept the property and the family together during the father's lifetime.

Another solution was the "sibling exchange marriage," in which two or more children of one family married into the same other family. The family of Thomas Wetmore, a Middletown proprietor, provides an extreme example of the use of this type of marriage. He had seventeen children by three wives over a period of thirty-four years; fifteen survived to adulthood, nine boys and six girls. Five of his children married into the Nathaniel Bacon family, two married the children of Samuel Stow and two more the children of Thomas Stow. When four of his sons established themselves in Middlefield in

the early eighteenth century, they already had ties of kinship and reciprocal obligation with three other families living in the town. These bonds between settler families could be reinforced in the next generation. Marriage between cousins was a third solution.

By the mid-nineteenth century, it appears that every man you met in Middlefield was either a Miller or a Coe. Indeed, by this point many marriages within the community were between sixth generation descendants of "Governor" Benjamin Miller. These traditional marriage and inheritance practices sustained the village for almost one hundred years, but by the nineteenth century, the maximum number of families

This pastoral photograph was taken by Dr. Robert L. Dickinson circa 1889. Courtesy Middlesex County Historical Society

E. Frank Coe's horse barn and trotting track. The fields now contain housing called Race Track Hollow. Courtesy Ray Hubbard

The Elias Coe House on Powder Hill Road. Courtesy Ray Hubbard

An example of a whaleback house, this one built in 1740 and demolished in 1901. Courtesy Middlefield Historical Society

the village could accommodate in this traditional pattern had been reached and the closely knit community began to unravel. Fathers could no longer provide enough land for all their sons. Some sons had to leave the village and seek new opportunities elsewhere. Their traditional way of life was coming to an end.

Early Architecture

In contrast to the growing sophistication of houses in more urban areas, the houses that were built by Middlefield farmers well into the nineteenth century followed basic Colonial forms. In the early Colonial period, architects were still unknown. The Colonial house form, however, was not unplanned, but was based on geometric proportions which give the New England "plain style" its pleasing uniform appearance regardless of the size of the structure. Both the structural standards for house building and the measurement of land were based on agricultural traditions. Early dwellings housed both people and animals; the separate cow barn came later. The sixteen-foot bay, which became a standard unit of house construction, could accommodate two teams of oxen.

The bay of the early houses was also known as a "bent" as very early wood frame construction used bent trees or "crucks" which extended in one continuous timber from the foundation to the ridgeline of the roof. Due to the scarcity of wood in Tudor England, the "cruck" form of construction was replaced by the post-and-beam type of framing, primarily because it used less wood. This style of framing persisted in the New World because it conserved material and because the basic structure could be laid out on the ground, the joints pegged together with "trunnels" or tree nails, by one man, who would need help only to raise the frame.

In Middlefield, this framing style was used until after the Civil War. It first appeared in the "lean-to," commonly called a saltbox. The oldest houses remaining in town today built by early settlers and their sons were built in this manner. Another feature of these houses was the overhang, another holdover from England. In these houses a logical and balanced floor plan surrounding a massive central chimney stack evolved. The size of the stack, however, did not allow much space for the entry "porch" as the front hall was then called, or the staircase to the second floor, nor did it permit access to any room except by passing through

Although he lived his adulthood in Meriden, Levi E. Coe was born in Middlefield and was active in community affairs there, including being Judge of Probate for many years. In February 1892, after deciding that Middlefield needed a library, Coe purchased one-sixth acre of land from Rebecca Moore in Middlefield Center. The Richardson Romanesque style brownstone structure, shown here standing alone, was built and dedicated in 1893. At a later date, the former St. Paul's Church stood beside it, as shown in the second photograph, and was joined to the library by an addition, as shown in the third photograph. The first and second photographs are courtesy Middlefield Historical Society and the third photograph is courtesy Bernadette S. Prue.

another room. While this plan was well-suited to communal living patterns, it constrained movement and allowed little individual privacy. The later center hall plan, sometimes called the Georgian floor plan, allowed people to pass through the house without going through another room. The front doorway opened on a long hall with doors opening into individual rooms and the "porch" moved to the exterior of the house, affording members of the family a degree of privacy which reflected a change in lifestyle. These Georgian and later Federal period houses were responding to a different view of the family and a rise in individualism.

It appears, however, that Middlefield families were content to live as their fathers and grandfathers had. Despite the general increase in population after the Revolution, so many young men left the village that few new houses needed to be built. The one family member left behind would live with the parents until they died before taking over the old homestead.

While families in Middlefield continued to live in these simple Colonial houses, and indeed to replicate them in the few new houses built shortly after the Revolution, more elaborate mansions were being built in Middletown as early as 1782 (de Koven House). Not until 1815 do we find any attempt to build such fashionable houses in Middlefield. The few Georgian central hall houses that were built were basically the same five-bay house form with a few

Georgian details. The only real architectural feature that characterizes such houses, built by several of the Coes, was the three-part Palladian window over the doorway and some very simple Georgian detail. The only one remaining today is the Elihu Coe House on Jackson Hill Road.

After the Revolution

Great changes took place in Middlefield in the years following the Revolution. Like their fathers and grandfathers before them, the young men who came of age then expected to carry on the traditions of this farming community: to receive land from their fathers, marry a girl from Middlefield, and live out their lives on land that had been in their families for almost a hundred years. The reality proved to be quite different. Some would be forced by circumstances to leave the community, becoming farmers where land was more abundant. Others would seek their fortunes in the cities as artisans, mechanics, or merchants. Even those who stayed in Middlefield would find their lives radically changed by forces largely beyond their control.

The unrest of the post-Revolutionary period was not generated simply by the war and the acute economic distress of its aftermath. Population pressures were acute; by 1790, 120 families were living in Middlefield, approximately 60 people per square mile. Even sons of settler families were beginning to feel the effects of population pressure. Their land had also been divided through three generations. Land in Middlefield was becoming scarce and valuable. Faced with prospects of impoverishment or prolonged dependency on fathers unwilling to part with remaining land, many began to look elsewhere for new opportunities.

At first these opportunities seemed to beckon from the nearby frontier, in the highlands of Connecticut and Massachusetts and later in Upper New York State and Ohio. A steady drain of young men from the village beginning soon after the Revolution continued through the early years of the nineteenth century. By 1815 over a third of the young had left Middlefield and the population was at its lowest point since before the war. Farming was on the decline by the early nineteenth century. As late as 1790, 90 percent of the young men in Middlefield

Beautiful countryside along Cherry Hill Road and Main Street in Rockfall, with the Coginchaug River in the background. Courtesy Ray Hubbard

143

Miss Mary Lyman with some friends. Courtesy Middlefield Historical Society

In 1911 this road passed by Henry Lyman's, between what is now the Lyman Apple Barrel Farm Store and Cooper Thermometer. Courtesy Middlefield Historical Society

Right: Toddler Oliver Bridgeman Lyman. Courtesy Middlefield Historical Society

were farmers like their fathers; by 1840 less than half were.

Those who stayed in farming had to seek new ways to use the land. The Great Embargo and the War of 1812, which temporarily closed the Port of Middletown and ultimately ended its commercial success, closed off one of the major outlets for farm products in the area. The economy of Middlefield was directly affected and land values declined. The grand list had dropped by 50 percent from late eighteenth-century levels and continued to decline through 1830.

There also appears to have been a major ecological crisis involving the disappearance of fish from the Connecticut River and the destruction of wheat agriculture by the Hessian fly blight.

The forests had also become depleted. In 1816, the year there was no summer, heavy frosts and snow in July and August destroyed the crops.

Within a few decades the Midwest came to dominate the market for grain production, shipping its crops eastward along the rivers and the new canals. Middlefield farmers responded by seeking new crops to grow. As Middletown and Meriden became more urbanized, local demand for farm products increased. Raising sheep became more important as New England's textile industry developed. By 1826 Middlefield led the country in sheep production. Orchards had been part of most eighteenth-century farms; Isaac Miller grew enough apples to produce cider at his mill. Later in the nineteenth century, Curtis Coe developed the famous Coe transparent cherry. Large-scale production of fruit began in the late nineteenth century by the Augur family. Today it is one of Middlefield's major products.

Of the young men who left town, the story of Phineas Miller, the son of Isaac Miller the apple-grower, is one of the most fascinating. One of the first Middlefield men to receive a college degree, Phineas

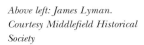

Above left: James Lyman. Courtesy Middlefield Historical Society

Above right: "On road to Middlefield Depot" from Durham over the Coginchaug River near the Lyman House. Courtesy Ray Hubbard

Below: Horses were common power sources on the Lyman Farm. Courtesy Middlefield Historical Society

The David B. Miller House near the Old North Burying Ground. *Courtesy Middlefield Historical Society*

traveled to Georgia upon graduation to serve as tutor to the children of General Nathanael Greene, who had been given a plantation there in recognition of his Revolutionary War service. When Greene died, Phineas married his widow and was apparently very successful at raising cotton and indigo. Together with Eli Whitney he developed the cotton gin, a fact that is not well known. Not everyone who left Middlefield was successful, however. David B. Miller wrote the following tragic tale from Whitestown, New York, to his brother Hezekiah in Middlefield:

David and Elias Just taken both lost their Reason. Aday is but Just Alive Ezra is some better after 20 days but has Esepearinced Everything but Death, Halsey I have sent away in short I believe it equals any house in New York where the putrid fever rages. Nothing but Destruction on Every quarter. Mrs. Miller and Rhoday Both worn out With Attendance on the sick. As for myself I don't expect to escape. 2 doctors one from

Whitestown at Present Attend and I Expect this to be the Last from your Brother.

> *Faire Well*
> *David B. Miller*

In addition to letters from distant relatives, diaries kept by those who stayed at home are valuable sources of information about life in early Middlefield. Joshua Stow, the second son of Elihu Stow, began his diary on his 21st birthday in 1783, recording his experiences as a farm boy, a miller's helper, and a schoolteacher, as well as his separate—and simultaneous—courtship of two young women, Olive Beckley of Berlin, and his cousin Ruth Coe, whom he eventually married.

Later in life Joshua encountered unusual challenges. Working for the election of Thomas Jefferson in 1800 earned him two federal appointments in Middletown, a directorship of the First Federal Bank of the United States, and the

146

postmastership. As a state senator he wrote the section of the revised state constitution of 1818 which finally disestablished the Congregational Church in Connecticut. When he died in 1842 he owned hundreds of acres of land and an estate worth over $20,000, but legal problems plagued him, the state of Connecticut confiscated most of his property, and his widow Ruth, who was to have received his house, land, and yearly dividends of cash, was eventually left with only the furniture. His lifespan covered the years of greatest change in the village. By the end of his lifetime, Middlefield's role and that of her citizens in the affairs of Middletown had substantially ended, although the growing separation between the communities was not formalized until 1866 when Middlefield was incorporated as a separate town.

Industrial Development

In contrast to Joshua Stow, other men found a different kind of opportunity right in Middlefield. Having exploited the land for over one hundred years, they turned to their other major natural resource, waterpower, establishing "manufactories" near the natural falls in the northeastern section, still known as Rockfall, and in the southern part of town, Baileyville. Ruins of many failed industrial ventures, some successful for quite a long period, remain today along streams in these areas. Stone foundations, washed out rock or earth dams, and depressions where the mill races diverted the water can be found at sites that date back to the original water rights and "privileges" granted to the first settlers with their land.

The right to dam a stream and build a mill was considered valuable property and was sold or handed down from father to son. When Benjamin Miller gave his son Ichabod 120 acres of land in 1734, for example, the property included the "liberty of flowing" (water rights), but Benjamin reserved the southeast corner of the property for his own mill.

Quite often, more than one operation took place at the same privilege. These included in the Colonial period saw, grist, and fulling mills. Although the heavier timbers used in framing houses continued to be hewn by hand, water-powered sawmills were a welcome replacement to the ancient custom of pit sawing. The gristmill, which eliminated the time-consuming hand grinding process needed to turn grain into flour, was the heart of any Colonial community, and inducements were offered to anyone who would

Top: This crossroads at what is now Route 147, Way Road, High Street, and Powder Hill Road, bordered the sites of numerous businesses over the years on the Beseck River. Courtesy Ray Hubbard.

Bottom: The building to the right was called the "Beehive." The main road curved between the buildings. Courtesy Ray Hubbard

147

The Russell Company complex.
Courtesy Ray Hubbard

establish such a mill. Fullers were also needed to dress the hand-woven woolen cloth and they utilized water power to run machinery to beat the cloth with fuller's earth. Two more unusual, but still traditional uses, were Shaler's snuff mill and downstream by the Falls, a powder mill run by a Durham man, Mr. Curtis.

Although it had become standard practice to keep the chemicals used in making blasting and gun powder in separate buildings at the site to reduce the hazard, powder making was still a dangerous business. Both the Curtis Mill and the later Vine Starr's Mill, which supplied blasting powder for the Portland quarries, were eventually destroyed by explosions.

In the 1790s a paper mill was established in Rockfall, and for a time this area was known as the Paper Mill Quarter. Waterpower was used to mix the rags and chemicals in large vats but the rest of the operation was done by hand. Eventually other men were able to mechanize the entire process, and the mill owners, Hubbard and Starr, went out of business. In the same period a slitting mill was started by Jehosaphat Stow. Previously, nails had been stamped out, slit from sheets of iron and headed by hand. Stow is credited with combining the two operations and producing nails made entirely by machine.

Baileyville and Rockfall

In the post-Civil War period Middlefield managed to combine vigorous industrial development with relative freedom from the poverty and social ills that accompanied such development in larger places. The population grew substantially in this period, fueled primarily by the arrival of industrial laborers who were often immigrants. Housing was adequate, living conditions were healthier than in the cities, industrial activity was never dominated by a single manufacturer or a single product, and farming continued to be one of the town's main activities.

The development of Baileyville really began in 1848 with the building of the Lake Beseck dam to provide a constant and controllable flow of water for the factories downstream. It was built by A. M. Bailey for $2,000 with local brownstone brought to the site by oxen from the nearby quarry on Powder Hill. Oliver Bailey, the father of this family, came to Middlefield from Haddam in the late eighteenth century and married into the Wetmore family; his children married into the Coe family. It is not surprising that one of the first companies established after the building of the dam was the Button Factory built by Andrew Coe and Alfred Bailey in 1849, a company that continued to make the same product until 1880. Both owners lived nearby, Andrew on Main Street and Alfred on Baileyville Road.

Other new men came to town attracted by the industrial potential in Baileyville. Moses Terrill moved to Middlefield, bought a substantial amount of land, and joined with David Lyman and his father William to found the Metropolitan Washing Machine Company, to manufacture a clothes wringer invented by Terrill and John Couch. The village of Baileyville grew up around this company. Terrill's brother William built a store, which remained in business as Fowler's Market until it was destroyed by fire in the 1980s.

The success of the Washing Machine Company can be attributed to one man, David Lyman II, the great-grandson of John Lyman, who had come to Middlefield from Durham in 1741 and purchased land from the Coe family. Through his efforts and his connections in the major financial centers of the country, the company's product reached a national market. Under his leadership the company established a sales office and showroom in New York City. He also recognized the need for a railroad to connect Middletown with New Haven, New York, and Boston. As the Air Line Railroad's first president, he supervised its construction from New Haven to Willimantic. Quite naturally he made sure that depots were built in his native town to make it easier to ship his company's products. The final step in the construction was the bridging of the Connecticut River at Middletown and the line opened in July 1871. David did not live to see the line in operation as he died, at age fifty-one, in January of that year.

Near the end of David Lyman's life, two major events took place, the end of the

The Rockfall Cotton Shop complex. During the 1938 hurricane, their generator (in the building with the smokestack) provided emergency power for the town. This flume along Cherry Hill Road carried water from the Coginchaug River to the Cotton Shop complex. Courtesy Ray Hubbard

Above left: This photograph shows the North District School at Jackson Hill Road and School Street in Middlefield. Courtesy Ray Hubbard

Above right: Central School in Middlefield circa 1927. Courtesy Middlefield Historical Society

South School, built in 1854 in Middlefield, is shown between the photographs of Miss Hattie North and Mrs. Lena Whitmore Greenbacker, teachers. The school became a private home in 1927. This South School class was photographed on March 21, 1911. The exterior is courtesy Middlefield Historical Society and the interior is courtesy Ray Hubbard.

Civil War and the incorporation of the town. There is a record of two Civil War veterans, Martin Moon and Edgar Nettleton, using their severance pay to buy property and houses in town. The war had financial implications for the town as well. Connecticut was saddled with six million dollars in war debt, to be paid by the towns and cities of the state. When Middlefield incorporated in 1866, the town assumed responsibility for one-tenth of Middletown's indebtedness.

Middlefield was the last of the satellite parishes to incorporate as a town. Although this separation may have been precipitated by the expectations of Middletown that the growing wealth in Middlefield could be tapped to pay a good part of the war debt, it was also promoted by the new industrialists in town, who recognized that Middlefield was no longer economically or socially dependent on the parent city. The influx of new men and new money, in combination with Yankee ingenuity, had made the town independent and financially secure. By the time the town was incorporated its political leaders included new men like Terrill, Couch, and Bailey as well as representatives of the old families, the Coes, Birdseys, Augurs and Millers.

The Lymans are notably absent from this list. Following in the family tradition of

Below: The Rockfall District School, shown on a 1907 postcard, had Miss Gilhannon for a teacher. The gentleman shown in front is unidentified.

Below: The Rockfall District School class in 1923. In the front row are: Ida Schaub, Mary Coleman, Stephen Mysling, Katherine Shrines, Sophie Otfinoski, Josephine Jagoda, and Mary Churen. In the second row are: Walter Shinkeffic, Mariano Passinese, John Bugai, Agnes Makuch, Cardine Rembis, Martha Stevens, Edward Makuch, Nellie Coleman, Jennie Coleman, Awnie Swaskoz, and Jennie Shinkeffic. In the third row are: Miss Bradley, Viola Geffken, Haviland Francisco, Walter Kokoszka, and Joseph Corona. In the fourth row are: Josephine Passinese, Josephine Slocum, Steffa Bankoszka, Steffa Kokoszka, John Otfinoski, Esther Behrens, and Annie Passinese. In the back row are: Robert Miller, Martin Konefal, David Steffman, Adolph Makuch, and Melvin Kavanaugh. Courtesy Ray Hubbard

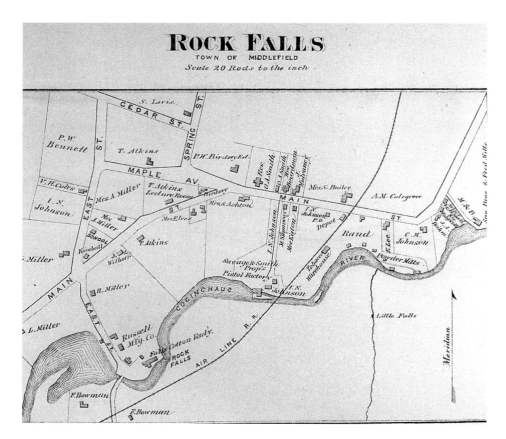

ROCK FALLS
TOWN OF MIDDLEFIELD
Scale 20 Rods to the inch

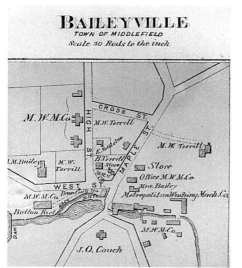

BAILEYVILLE
TOWN OF MIDDLEFIELD
Scale 30 Rods to the inch

not being directly involved in politics, William, the son of David Lyman, concentrated on business. With his father's capital and the railroad already in town, he was in an advantageous position not only to carry on the family business but to develop his own inventions, which became the basis of the Lyman Gunsight Corporation. The company remained under the Lyman family's direct control until 1969, supplying scopes and gunsights to the U.S. Army in three wars.

Many of the factory workers who lived in Baileyville and Rockfall were immigrants. Among them were the Irish who came to the United States following the repeated failures of the potato crop in Ireland. A number of Irish families also settled in Middlefield, and by 1890 they had established their own church in town.

Italian immigrants followed the Irish beginning in the very late nineteenth century. One house in Middlefield can still be identified with these later immigrants, the Salvatore Augeri House on Main Street. The only dwelling known to have been built by an early Sicilian immigrant in town, its brick facade reflects its owner's origins.

A large influx of newcomers from Central Europe began in the early twentieth century, as Polish immigrants came to the Connecticut River Valley in

Lake Beseck Dam circa 1889. Courtesy Middlefield Historical Society

Mud Pond Dam near the railroad trestle. Courtesy Middlefield Historical Society

search of cheap land and jobs, establishing communities in many of Connecticut's major cities. One of the first to arrive in Middlefield was John Piehota (Pehota) who built several unusual houses of his own design in Rockfall on Main Street. These men worked nearby in factories on the Coginchaug, particularly in the Rogers Manufacturing Company, established in 1891 on the site of Miller and Bennett's bone and sawmill, which had been in operation since 1868. Although Middlefield's Poles never built their own church (they attended mass at St. Mary's in Middletown), they did form a Tadeusz Kosciuszko Society and established a significant community in Rockfall.

Nineteenth-Century Architecture

Both the Rockfall and Baileyville neighborhoods grew rapidly in the last half of the nineteenth century. Earlier houses were interspersed with modest dwellings of later design but still reminiscent of the Colonial house form. Few of the houses built in Middlefield in the late nineteenth century made any concession to popular fashion.

By mid-century few houses were still being built with the ancient method of post-and-beam framing. With steam and water turbines now perfected, sawmills could turn out large quantities of sawn and

LAKE BESECK, FROM BATHING BEACH, MIDDLEFIELD, CONN.

Above: Lake Beseck has been a popular beach for many years. Courtesy Fran Korn

Right: The pedals may be a little hard for her to reach on this road grader, shown in front of the Lake Beseck Club House. Courtesy Ray Hubbard

"A. W. Bailey and Andrew Coe formed a company in order to manufacture buttons. They were located just below the present Beseck Dam. To their dismay many times during the year, the water supply was not adequate for power so they organized a company to build a dam. The foundation was laid on sixteen feet of solid stone mostly taken from Powder Hill. Apparently some was from where the dinosaur tracks are now located and from the quarry known as the Fowler & Coe pit. Bailey's history mentions much about the beautiful tracks in some of the slabs and they tried to save the best ones for the top so that they might show. Also was mentioned that a formation was taken out in the shape of a nest about six inches deep by four feet in diameter which showed an impression very much like three large eggs. This was laid to one side of the dam to be taken to Wesleyan University. That night a severe storm hit, and the banks fell in, so the slab was lost in the lake. This dam was completed in 1848. In 1852 this dam was raised five feet for more water supply and again in 1870, another five feet was added, for a total thirty-seven feet.

"The Button Shop was completed in 1849 having a very large overshot water wheel. Soon after this Andrew Coe started to raise large sums for the company but left for the west taking the money with him. He was not satisfied but still acquired more money for the same purpose out there and left with that. This left Mr. Bailey to meet these large obligations therefore he lost the company, home, furnishings and all items of any value. Penniless he started over again. Mr. David Lyman offered him a job in his mill and gave him a cow. This mill of Mr. Lyman's was built in 1855 and stood on the left bank as you cross the little bridge over Beseck River going towards the center. A wooden conduit ran water from the dam on the west side of the railroad, under the railroad to the shop close under the railroad embankment on the property now owned by Cahill. Also where the water way crossed, the turning and wagon shop located on property now owned by M. Tucker. It states that he was noted for his ability to sharpen mill stones.

"In 1857 Mr. David Lyman began to manufacture the Metropolitan Washing Machine. At this point the writer would like to call attention to the fact that as shown on the old map of Middlefield there was a building marked at this location belonging to the Metropolitan Washing Machine. This would indicate that this business was started in this location and then expanded in the large three story building known as the Metropolitan Manufacturing Company. Said Mr. Bailey did improve these items which Mr. Lyman was promoting. It seems that a Mr. Dickerson from Vermont had made improvements as well as Mr. Bailey and Mr. Lyman who bought them and started in a big way to make wringers. He took in Mr. Moses W. Terrill and formed the Metropolitan Washing Machine Company.

"After Mr. Lyman's death the name was changed to Metropolitan Manufacturing Company. It also mentions the Mr. John O. Couch worked with them on much of the developments. This was in addition to Mr. Couch making many items such as candle sticks of iron and a special designed gun for the protection of one's property. It was designed so that when properly hooked up to a door and any one trying to enter would get shot." (taken from an old text) Courtesy Ray Hubbard

dressed lumber of uniform size. The balloon framing method was invented and machine-made nails were readily available. The single most important effect of the balloon frame was freedom of design. Floor plans were no longer restricted to simple rectangles; houses were no longer simply boxes with a roof. The styles of the Victorian period made the most of this new flexibility. This was also the era when the average family could afford a Victorian cottage; smaller in scale, perhaps, than the mansions built by the wealthy, but similar in style.

Despite these developments, however, and in contrast to the elaborate Victorian mansions being built in other towns, Couch, Terrill, and several Baileys built simple frame dwellings with little architectural embellishment. Indeed, with few exceptions, most of the architectural styles that we associate with this era—Queen Anne, Stick-Style, Gothic Revival, and Italianate—were never popular in Middlefield. Even one of the most imposing houses built in town by one of the most progressive citizens, David Lyman, is basically still an eighteenth-century Georgian house, framed by post-and-beam, its only concession to fashion the use of ornament derived from several of the newer architectural styles.

Given the architectural evidence, it is tempting to assume that Middlefield was a relatively classless society in this period, a sort of rural utopia, but this was clearly not the case. Although living conditions were probably better in Middlefield than in the cities, the new immigrants were still relatively poor, particularly when they first arrived. There may have been fewer paupers in town, but there certainly was enough wealth for men to build elaborate houses if they chose to do so. The absence of ostentatious displays of this wealth had to be deliberate. Rural attitudes may have played a part: rejection of "new fangled notions" and a highly developed sense of Yankee thrift. The old families' sense of themselves may also have been involved. Members of the old families had no need to impress anyone with their status; in a town this size, everyone already was well aware of the position they occupied.

Top: The Moses Terrill House burned in 1909. Courtesy Ray Hubbard

Bottom: Burnham's Store on Way Road, which later became the original Fowler's Market. The "new" Fowler's Market (shown circa 1978) burned in 1988. Courtesy Ray Hubbard

The Metropolitan Washing Machine Company in Baileyville (now Route 147 and Way Road) began by making washing machines, but later switched to wringers when they became more profitable. The pipe shown in this recent photograph brought water from Lake Beseck to the Wringer Shop along the Beseck River (now called the Ellen Doyle Brook). The last photograph shows the workforce in the late 1800s.

Left: Courtesy Bernard Prue

Middle right: Courtesy Ray Hubbard

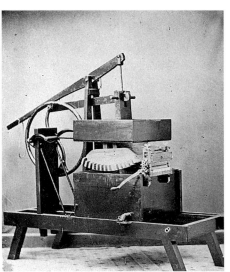

Middle left: Courtesy Middlefield Historical Society

Below left: Courtesy Middlefield Historical Society

Below right: Courtesy Middlefield Historical Society

157

Main Street Rockfall in the early 1900s. Courtesy Ray Hubbard

Main Street in Rockfall was still a dirt road when this coal-burning locomotive passed by the Railroad Depot. Courtesy Ray Hubbard

Perhaps in the final analysis, Middlefield men remained farmers at heart. With almost two centuries of agrarian tradition behind them, they were more comfortable with houses that owed more to traditional values than to popular taste.

Geographically insular, Middlefield grew at its own pace and in its own way. Despite its participation in the Industrial Revolution, it remained essentially rural, and traditional patterns lingered on. Nowhere is this more evident than in the architecture of the town. What little modern development that has taken place has not disturbed the pastoral quality of this rural scene, which is still one of Middlefield's chief assets. Few of the houses that remain today are still owned by descendants of the original builders. The buildings still stand, however, to remind us of Middlefield's heritage.

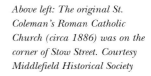

Above left: The original St. Coleman's Roman Catholic Church (circa 1886) was on the corner of Stow Street. Courtesy Middlefield Historical Society

Above right: The Middlefield Town Hall still stands in the center of town. Courtesy Ray Hubbard

Shown is Mr. Lyman inspecting one of the newly made gunsights. On the right is the building housing the Telescope Sight Division of the company. Courtesy Ray Hubbard

159

*Above: William Lyman is shown
holding a boat with his bow-
facing rowing gears installed.
Courtesy Middlefield Historical
Society*

*Right: The Lyman
Manufacturing Company is
still in business, although it has
moved to Middletown. They made
diverse products, including Bow-
facing Rowing Gear. Courtesy
Ray Hubbard*

Bow-Facing Rowing Gear.

Above left: The Pistol Shop was built in 1881 by Otis Smith. It was known for manufacturing the Smith revolver. Courtesy Middlefield Historical Society

Above right: The T. Lindemark Store and Post Office in Rockfall, circa 1957. In the car are the Magee boys and friends. Courtesy Ray Hubbard

Middle: Rodowic's Store in Rockfall. The sign reads "Buy this flour because Pillsbury's Best." Courtesy Ray Hubbard

Below: The Rogers Manufacturing Company. Courtesy Ray Hubbard

Mr. Clair L. Huse was manager of the Middlefield Grain & Coal Company. Mr. Harry Link, Sr. is shown behind the counter in this well-stocked country store. Courtesy Ray Hubbard

Above right: Dr. Robert L. Dickinson took this photograph of the Sarah Dickinson House circa 1889. Miss Jeannie Dickinson is at the easel. Courtesy Middlesex County Historical Society

Above left: Former Middlefield Post Office. Courtesy Ray Hubbard

Middle right: The E. C. Strickland House on Powder Hill Road. Courtesy Middlefield Historical Society

Middle left: The High Street birthplace of Grace Augusta Bigelow circa 1905. Courtesy Middlefield Historical Society

Below: Albert Moush and Albert Hall (without hat) pose in front of their market, the A. D. Emmons Meat Market, on High Street in Middlefield circa 1917. Courtesy Ray Hubbard

*Above left: The Lyman Barn.
Courtesy Ray Hubbard*

*Above right: The Lyman cattle
barn was built in 1916 and
destroyed by fire November 17,
1965. Courtesy Ray Hubbard*

*Middle: The Middlefield-
Middletown Trolley stopped at
Rockfall with conductors Jack
Kidney and Patsy Quirk. Mrs.
Mary Warzecha is just stepping
off. Courtesy Ray Hubbard*

*Below: The Middlefield Railroad
Station on West Street. Courtesy
Ray Hubbard*

164

Left: A train leaving the station, with Aaron Miller's house on the left. Courtesy Middlefield Historical Society

Below: Support for the Middlefield Volunteer Fire Department. Courtesy Ray Hubbard

Route 66 (Meriden Road) west of Guida's. Courtesy Middlefield Historical Society

The Peckham family was famous for their gladiolus fields. Peckham Field was named in their honor. Courtesy Ray Hubbard

Above: "Annies get your guns"
—we can only wonder what the
occasion was. Courtesy
Middlefield Historical Society

Left: Jaunty transportation for
a Sunday drive. Unfortunately,
the handsome couple could not be
identified. Courtesy Ray Hubbard

6
Portland

Portland's history cannot be separated from the history of the two towns of which it once formed a part: Middletown and East Hampton. However, by the end of its first 130 years, Portland had acquired a character distinctly different from both, which finally led to its incorporation as a separate political, economic, and social entity by the end of the nineteenth century.

The western half of the land which now forms East Hampton, and most of the land which now forms the eastern half of Portland, were distributed in 1674. This extensive tract formed the major part of the allotment known as the "Great Lotts."

Blacksmith shop at the Brainerd Quarry circa 1885, with the Connecticut River in the background.

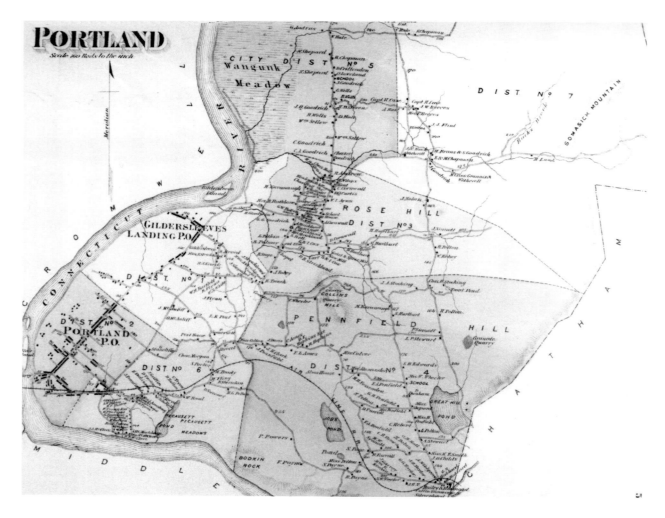

PORTLAND
Scale 160 Rods to the inch

Courtesy Jim Sarbaugh

These lots stretched two and one-half miles from east to west, ran south from the Glastonbury line to the Haddam line, and north from the Haddam line on the western side of the river to the Maromas section of Middletown. Forty of the fifty-two lots (corresponding to the fifty-two original proprietors) were on the east side of the river. Most of the remaining land in Portland was reserved for use by the Indians. Land records indicate that this reservation was located in and around the area which now comprises the village of Gildersleeve.

No significant settlement of "East Middletown" began until the turn of the eighteenth century. When the inhabitants of the area had signed an agreement to build their first meetinghouse on Hall Hill in 1710, the entire eastern half of

Middletown was populated by only twenty-seven families. This area was in a very real sense "the wilderness" for those living in Middletown during the seventeenth and early eighteenth centuries. Many natural physical hardships and practical difficulties, such as traveling back to Middletown across the "Great River" for mandatory weekly gatherings at the meetinghouse or to acquire goods and implements which they were unable to provide for themselves, probably served to deter all but the hardiest in the first few years.

In 1736 the residents of what eventually became Portland petitioned the town of Middletown for establishment as a separate town. While this initial attempt failed, interest in the idea grew as more settlers arrived. In 1767 another petition was submitted to the Connecticut General Assembly. This petition by the new township of Chatham, as it was called, was granted with the limitation that there be only one representative from the town to the General Assembly. Local tradition holds that the name referred to the shipbuilding port of Chatham, England, and was selected because of the shipbuilding activity which had already begun along the riverbank in Middle Haddam and in the Wangunk Meadows.

Not long after the establishment of Chatham, a movement began to subdivide the town further. The first complaints were voiced by residents living south of the Salmon River, who not only had to travel ten miles to town meetings, but also had to ford the Salmon River. In 1795 they petitioned the town of Chatham not to oppose their efforts to gain sanction from the General Assembly to be annexed by the town of Haddam. While Chatham opposed their secession, the town took the matter under consideration and at the same meeting proposed the construction of a bridge to link this area with the rest of the town. This bridge, which was constructed in 1792 and was subsequently rebuilt a number of times, still stands. Now

known as the Comstock Bridge, it is one of the few covered bridges remaining in Connecticut.

The bridge did not fully satisfy the demands of residents south of the Salmon River, who persisted in their efforts to secede. The General Assembly finally granted their request in 1830. The final subdivision of Chatham divided the town into the present towns of Portland and East Hampton, which retained the name Chatham until the early twentieth century. The first efforts to effect this division began in 1788. In 1841 the question was finally settled when the General Assembly officially incorporated the town of Conway, which several minutes later was renamed Portland, in reference to the English town renowned for its high quality building stone.

Penfield Hill and Rose Hill District

Roughly bounded by Job's Pond Road to the west and Great Hill Road and the East Hampton town line to the east, Penfield Hill is Portland's rural southeastern district. This area was settled

Courtesy Jim Sarbaugh

Two views of the picturesque mill buildings at Cox's Falls. Top: Courtesy Middlesex County Historical Society. Bottom: Courtesy Portland Public Library

very early in the eighteenth century. John and Ann (Cornwall) Penfield and their five children arrived in East Middletown in 1724. It was to be the home of the Chatham Penfields for the next two centuries.

Although the earlier settlers had to travel back across the Great River to attend church every Sunday for roughly twenty years before they erected their own meetinghouse on Hall Hill and became the Third Ecclesiastical Society of Middletown, the community that the Penfields came to settle included over thirty families and was big enough to support its own meetinghouse and ministers by 1721.

In addition to John Penfield and his wife Ann Cornwall, four other families came to settle on the eastern hills of present-day Portland. The Shepards, Stewarts, Browns, and Peltons intermarried with the Penfields and Cornwalls and formed a neighborhood in which nearly everyone was related. This six-family network is directly linked with nearly every historic house in the district today.

This pattern of intermarriage was not simply the result of proximity. Unless some attempt was made to maintain family farms intact through the careful control of marriage partners, the descendants of the first settlers would be forced to move onto new land or find another means of supporting themselves. They would first begin to settle in the outlying areas of the town on usually less desirable farming land, but finally would be forced to move further away to remoter parts of the colony.

Until the end of the nineteenth century, Penfield Hill was a farming community. Some of the residents had special skills even at the outset of the settlement in the 1720s, but it is unlikely that they were able to devote full time to any single craft or trade at first.

One of the early farmers known to have settled on Penfield Hill was Joseph Pelton. He was born in 1722 in Lyme, married Hannah Penfield in 1744, and lived in the Penfield Hill area from the time of his marriage. He and his wife had thirteen children. John Shepard (b. 1688) was another early resident of the area. He had a farm as early as 1725. Like his Hartford forebears, who had shops on Cooper Lane (now Lafayette Street), John Shepard was skilled in coopering. Families stored their winter supply of food and cider in barrels made by craftsmen like Shepard.

By the mid-eighteenth century, all of Connecticut was growing rapidly. On Penfield Hill there was a flurry of building. Three houses from this period are still

Courtesy Jim Sarbaugh

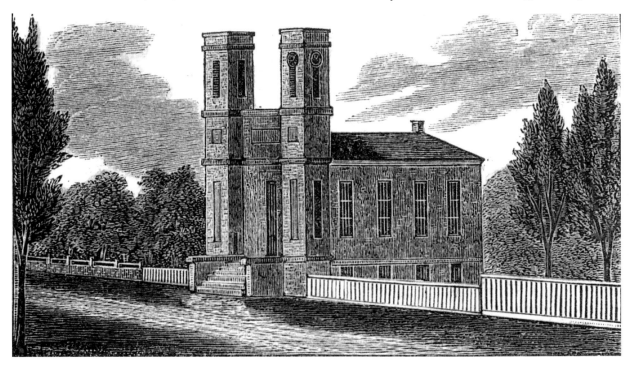

OLD FERRYBOAT "PORTLAND" 1888

The new town included the First Society (now Portland), East Hampton Society, and Middle Haddam Society. Although each community had its own Congregational Church by this time, town business for all of Chatham was conducted in the meetinghouse of the First Society.

Jonathan Penfield, the son of John and Ann Cornwall Penfield, was elected Town Clerk of Chatham at the town's inception. He served until his death in 1784, when his son Zebulon took over. In the 1790s Chatham erected a new "Town House," closer to East Hampton parish, but still in the First Society. It stood on the west side of Penfield Hill and served all of Chatham until 1841, when East Hampton and Portland split and the Episcopal Society gave their old meetinghouse on Bartlett Street to the town of Portland.

Ferryboat "Portland" Burned April 2, 1889

standing today (the first Daniel Shepard House, John Shepard House and Daniel Burton House).

As the eastern and western communities of Middletown grew, their differences became more pronounced. The Middletown side was becoming a mercantile center, while the Portland side held the majority of the farmers. Town government, administered from the west side, became increasingly unsatisfactory to those who lived on the east side. In 1767 East Middletown became a separate township and chose the name Chatham.

Toward the end of the eighteenth century the character of the agrarian Penfield Hill community had changed. At first a decentralized group of independent farms, Penfield Hill gradually developed a spirit of cooperation and specialization, fostered by the now well-established kinship networks. There were several craftsmen working in the late eighteenth and early nineteenth centuries, including Jesse Penfield, cooper; Samuel Penfield,

174

blacksmith; and Abner Pelton, part-time shoemaker as well as farmer.

In 1808 the Chatham and Colchester Turnpike was established. It ran from the ferry landing near the present Portland Bridge over eighteen miles to Colchester, passing the foot of Penfield Hill on the way. By the early nineteenth century the First Society of Chatham had 203 dwelling houses and two mercantile stores. Penfield Hill was one of seven school districts in Chatham and had fifty pupils that year. In addition to the "Town House," the tavern, the schoolhouse, several shops occupied by coopers, and several blacksmiths, the Penfield district had a tannery by 1815.

Penfield Hill Road may have been laid out early in the eighteenth century (probably about 1725, soon after the meetinghouse was finished during the flurry of East Middletown "road-laying"), but for the first hundred years of its existence it was simply "the highway" to the residents. Judging roughly by the number of dwelling houses, the whole town of Chatham seems to have doubled in size in the first half of the nineteenth century. In 1814, 203 dwelling houses were

listed as the total number for the First Society. In the census of 1850, 401 houses were counted. The growth of the town was partly due to the success of the quarry and shipbuilding industries which began in the first half of the nineteenth century.

The 1850 census shows that there were still more men engaged in farming than any other occupation. But of the twenty men listed, twelve were forty years old or considerably older. Most households had noticeably few sons over the age of fifteen living at home at the time of the census. Many young men had left the Connecticut River Valley to become part of the westward migration to new and fertile land. In larger towns, factory work had drawn many young men and women away from the farm since the early decades of the century. By the late 1800s, manufacturing concerns such as the U.S. Stamp Company had established factories employing up to 450 people in Portland.

By the turn of the twentieth century, Penfield Hill no longer had the large family farms that had flourished a century before. Agriculture in the district was small-scale and seldom the sole means of

The Rose Hill School was operated by Miss Dora Stocking until 1936, when it was replaced by the original Gildersleeve school. Courtesy Mr. & Mrs. Walter W. Olson

G.A.R. Veterans in front of Portland Civil War monument with Freestone band, 1885

support for a family. Many of the descendants of the six families which had once dominated the district had moved away. In 1920 the Penfield Hill schoolhouse was closed. The tavern and the "Townhouse" disappeared without a trace. Less than a dozen houses from the eighteenth and nineteenth centuries still stand in the district today.

Gildersleeve

The old streets of Gildersleeve are Main, Prospect, Summer, and Bartlett Streets, Indian Hill Avenue, and Ferry Lane. Gildersleeve displays nearly every style of vernacular architecture constructed from 1700 to the present. The area identified as Gildersleeve (bounded by the Connecticut River on the north and west) was originally made up of four of the so-called Half Mile Lots and a sizable portion of Indian territory.

Even before settlers came to live on the east side of the Great River, farming was carried on by Middletown and Upper Houses residents who supposedly returned home across the river (swam or rowed) at the end of the day. The earliest house in Gildersleeve was built around 1703 by Jonathan Warner, a former Middletown Upper Houses resident, whose wife was Elizabeth Ranney, granddaughter of a proprietor. The oldest house remaining in the Gildersleeve area is the Jonathan Warner House, incorporated into the house at 613 Main Street with additions in 1764 and 1912. The 1750 meetinghouse, constructed when the 1721 meetinghouse grew too small, was placed on land purchased from the Indians.

Shipbuilding had begun by 1756 when a petition to acquire the Indian territory referred to "Vessels" which had been built in the Indian Hill area, and others which would be built "directly" if the land could be purchased and a highway run through it.

176

The Revolutionary War provided a stimulus to the growth of Gildersleeve. The drive for military preparedness increased demand for ships. After the war, restrictions were lifted on the merchant marine and the demand grew for nonmilitary ships also. With the growth of shipbuilding came the development of associated industries: blacksmith's shops, coopers, a shoemaker, a fulling mill, and a distillery (something of a necessity considering that the shipyards had rum breaks just as twentieth-century office workers have coffee breaks). About this time the Chatham-Marlborough Turnpike was laid out, running up present-day Main Street, across Wangunk Meadows and out through Meshomasic.

Between 1776 and 1812, Gildersleeve gained approximately fifteen new houses. Gildersleeve carpenters, trained in the Colonial tradition and isolated in a small rural town, built central-chimney Colonial period houses all through the Georgian period (late 1700s) and into the Federal

period (1780–1820). Somehow the concept of stylishness seems to have been rejected in Gildersleeve until relatively late. Sylvester Gildersleeve's 1833 house on Main Street ushered in the Federal style in Gildersleeve. Gildersleeve, a rising shipbuilder, included a decorative fanlight in his gable-to-street, three-bay, side-hall house. Not until the late nineteenth

The Johnson family immigrated from Sweden and bought the Great Hill Road farm in 1890. Shown are Andrew Johnson and his sister, Judy, cutting and stacking wheat and harvesting tobacco in the 1920s. Courtesy Mr. & Mrs. Walter O. Olson

century was this area identified as Gildersleeve, a name adopted in his honor for having been instrumental in building up this area. Sylvester was born in 1795 in his father Phillip's house on Indian Hill. His father worked in the shipyards and ran a fulling mill, removing the lanolin from wool cloth. Gildersleeve married in 1814, only nineteen years old. He was virtually without means, so he left his young wife with her father and went to the Great Lakes to build boats for the War of 1812. However, the war ended before his boat was finished and Gildersleeve returned to Portland. With the little he had saved, he bought the house next door to his father's. He did some shipbuilding in Glastonbury and in 1821 Seth Overton hired him to build two ships. In 1824 Gildersleeve's wife died, about the time he began building ships at Churchill's Landing located further north in the Wangunk Meadow. By 1833, when he built his fairly elaborate house, Gildersleeve was doing well.

His success rippled down through the neighborhood by providing employment for others. In 1836 Samuel S. Buckingham established a general store on the corner of Main and Indian Hill. Across Main Street, Daniel Cheny ran a tavern in the 1830s and 1840s. This small intersection became a veritable commercial center.

Sylvester Gildersleeve won prosperity for his section of Portland by linking it to other growth areas in the town and eventually, the nation. He established a bond with the quarries by supplying the ships to transport their stone. His business contacts in New York and Texas proved profitable when the New York-Galveston Shipping Line was established. In 1836 the Gildersleeve yard built the William Bryan, the first vessel to sail as a regular packet from New York to Texas.

The architecture from the 1840s and 1850s, mostly Greek Revival and Italianate styles, indicates to some extent the prosperity of this period. At this time the Congregational Church, always near Gildersleeve, was relocated onto Main Street facing Bartlett Street. And, in 1855, Sylvester Gildersleeve built his new brick store, larger than the previous buildings and with its cupola and Italianate detailing, far more impressive.

The Civil War required boats, so Gildersleeve built the *Cayuga*, a five-hundred-ton steam gunboat, for the U.S. government. After the War, Gildersleeve began to diversify. He built a mattress factory and a wagon works on Indian Hill. He also bought up several of the older houses to rent to his workers and constructed what he referred to as the "Swede Tenement" (Indian Hill Avenue).

Tobacco had become a profitable cash crop for Portland farmers in the second half of the nineteenth century. Gildersleeve owned good tobacco land between Main Street and the river, an area that is still under cultivation today. Several other men who lived in the area also produced and marketed tobacco. Fewer houses were being built in this period, reflecting the gradual decline of industry in the area by the end of the nineteenth century.

The shipbuilding industry was declining. The demand for ships to carry brownstone waned as the popularity of brownstone as a building material declined. Although wooden hulls for transport ships were still being built during World War I and towed to New York to be completed and fitted out with marine engines, in 1932 the Gildersleeve yard produced its last ship, a coal barge named the *Jack Daley*, the 358th ship built by the Gildersleeves since their start in 1821.

Bucktown

The term "Bucktown" is today often used to denote much of the northeastern quarter of the town. The area was established as a separate school district in 1768. Known perhaps more appropriately through most of the 1800s as "Buck's Hollow," Bucktown proper lies in a small

Grace Mitchell Bacon was the wife of John Plumb
Bacon, president of the Middletown Savings
Bank and former owner of a funeral parlor. Born
in Portland, she died in her '90s (circa 1955)
and is buried behind the Episcopal Church there.
This Mitchell family photograph includes Mr. &
Mrs. Brown, Ira Brown, Mr. & Mrs. Mitchell,
Miss Grace Mitchell (center back of photograph),
Elizabeth Grainold, and Mrs. Walker. Grace
Mitchell's mother was born in this Greek Revival
home. Courtesy Nancy E. Schott

valley on the fringe of the western foothills of Somasic Mountain and the Meshomesic State Forest. The history of Bucktown begins with the settlement of James Buck (1774–1838), who built the first permanent dwelling known to have been erected in the hollow itself in 1799, a house which still stands along the eastern side of Cotton Hill Road slightly north of its intersection with Old Marlborough Turnpike.

The growth of the local shipbuilding industry played a pivotal role in the development of Bucktown. The increase in the demand for ships created a greater demand for milled lumber. Dense stands of oak and chestnut trees, combined with its location on an existing "major" road which ran from the northeast quarter to the river, made Bucktown an ideal location

for a sawmill. Bisecting the hollow, Reservoir Brook's relatively steep drop over a short distance and its high banks and narrow bed at various points along its course, were well-suited to dam construction. It is hardly surprising, therefore, that the first structure to have been built in Bucktown was a sawmill erected by Charles Churchill, a shipbuilder who established a building yard in the Wangunk Meadows about 1795.

Three years later, James Buck purchased a forty-acre piece of land in the area from his older brother Jeremiah, a shipjoiner who worked in the Churchill shipyard. The following year James, who was also working as a shipjoiner in the Churchill shipyard, purchased his employer's mill. For the next seventy years,

The turn-of-the-century Town Hall and Buck Library is shown before the north wing was added and in 1996 with the new wing in place. A new library was built behind the original structure. The older photograph is courtesy Middlesex County Historical Society and the newer is courtesy Bernadette S. Prue.

Buck's mill was one of the major suppliers of ship plank and house timber in the Middletown area.

Buck also pursued a number of other occupations, including carriage-making, inventing and patenting farm implements, and farming. Of these, the most significant, with the exception perhaps of lumbering, was his carriage-making operation; just when he established it is unclear. Several carriage shops and blacksmith and casting shops were standing on the property by the 1830s. While the mill appears to have been removed late in the nineteenth century, the remains of the dam and tail race are still visible in the ravine below the house built in 1847 by James Buck's fourth son, James F. Buck. All of James Buck's sons, including his youngest son Horace (for whom Portland's Town Library was named), followed in their father's footsteps in the carriage-making and lumbering businesses. Erastus for a number of years spent the winters in Wilmington, North Carolina, where he employed several workers in a similar carriage-shop operation. The Buck family's activity in North Carolina also seems to support a long-established local tradition that the "buckboard wagon," which figured so prominently as a mode of transportation in the South and East during the nineteenth century, was both designed by and named for this family of carriage makers from Portland. If the "buckboard" was indeed the product of the family's operations in Wilmington, it seems most likely that the credit for its design will eventually be traced to the creative and inventive mind of James F. Buck.

Today Bucktown is a peaceful little hollow located in a relatively thinly settled outlying rural area of town. With the exception of the five houses which now stand in this area, four of them built by members of the Buck family before 1847, and the existence of the Portland Reservoir, which was constructed about a half mile to the east in 1889, this section bears a closer resemblance to its seventeenth- and eighteenth-century appearance than any other part of town.

Quarries

Throughout Portland's history the brownstone quarries were a natural resource. Only in the nineteenth century, however, did the industry significantly affect the town's economic, social, and architectural development. The expansion and development of the industry depended on the brownstone itself, an influx of cheap labor provided by Irish immigration, a demand for brownstone in the major coastal cities of the country, and readily available ships to transport the product. By the late nineteenth century, the industry had made Portland distinctly different from the neighboring river towns of Cromwell and East Hampton.

The Early Years: 1650–1820

Portland was hardly unique in its extensive deposits of brownstone. The primary difference between the deposits in Portland and those in other communities, however, was that some of the brownstone in Portland lay exposed in outcroppings along the river when settlement began in the area in the 1650s. This made it more readily accessible to Middletown's early settlers.

But while the value of this resource was recognized early, extensive quarrying operations would not begin for more than a hundred years. Brownstone was used primarily in these early years for foundations, walls, and gravestones by residents of the lower Connecticut Valley, and most often by those in Middletown. While demand clearly existed outside Middletown as early as 1665, it was relatively small-scale, and, combined with

Loading quarry stone at the Connecticut River Dock. Courtesy Middlesex County Historical Society.

Right: Typical quarry equipment. Courtesy Cromwell Historical Society

the lack of effective methods for transporting large shipments of stone, quarrying was not very profitable before the 1730s. A house constructed for Thomas Hancock in Boston of "Middletown Stone," cut by Thomas Johnson of Middletown Upper Houses in 1736, is the first documented case of production of large amounts of brownstone for long-distance shipping.

By the end of the 1770s, demand for brownstone had increased to where quarrying began to rival farming as a principal occupation. Its economic importance eventually burgeoned to the point where, by 1840, it had become a major industry, far surpassing either farming or shipbuilding as the major economic force in Portland's development.

The history of the quarries as a modern industry began in 1783 with the formation of the commercial quarrying partnership of Hurlbut and Roberts. The partnership maintained operations until 1812, when the business was sold to Erastus and Silas Brainerd. The business was operated under the firm name of E.&S. Brainerd

until Silas' death in 1857, when it was renamed Erastus Brainerd and Company. It was finally incorporated as the Brainerd Quarry Company in 1884.

The second major firm established was the partnership formed by Nathaniel Shaler and Joel Hall in 1788. It continued to operate as Shaler and Hall until its merger with the Brainerd Company at the end of the nineteenth century. In 1819 a third company was formed by Daniel Russell and Robert Patten. Later known as Russell and Hall, the company was finally incorporated as the Middlesex Quarry Company in 1841. For three firms to become established in this relatively short period shows that market demand for brownstone had not only increased by the 1780s, but was continuing to grow throughout the early nineteenth century.

By the end of the second decade of the nineteenth century, Middletown was on the decline as a major port, causing a subsequent decline in demand for vessels produced in local shipyards. The one major exception was Portland. By 1840 the annual tonnage produced in Portland actually began to increase. In fact,

Portland quarries provided brownstone for many structures in New York and Boston. The quarry picture was taken by Fred Stancliff (see the octagon houses in Portland). Courtesy Middlesex County Historical Society

Locomotive of The Shaler & Hall Quarry Company, about 1896

Right: Constructed in 1888 for three sisters, the Brainerd House on Main Street was built of brownstone from the Brainerd, Shaler and Hall quarry. It is now called Stonehaven and is owned by Elmcrest Hospital. Courtesy Portland Public Library

Opposit page top: Courtesy Middlesex County Historical Society

Opposite page below: Derricks such as these were used to move the huge blocks of brownstone that were quarried in Portland in the 1800s. The river and Middletown church spires can be seen in the background. Notice the workmen on the center right. Courtesy Bernard Prue

184

Oxen used at Brainerd Quarry, 1884

shipbuilding remained significant in the town's economy until the end of the nineteenth century, and did not totally die out until the 1930s.

To some degree this paradox resulted from the entrepreneurial skills of the prominent, nineteenth-century shipyard owner, Sylvester Gildersleeve. Gildersleeve established and maintained markets for his ships in an era when most other local shipbuilders failed. The major reason for his success was his connection with Portland's growing nineteenth-century brownstone quarrying industry. An examination of Sylvester Gildersleeve's probate records shows that he owned substantial stock in each of the town's major nineteenth-century firms. There is also little question as to the important market which the quarry industry provided for Gildersleeve as a shipbuilder.

Fifty-six percent of Gildersleeve's ships were involved in quarry-related business.

Expansion and Immigration

By mid-century the quarry companies were responding to new demand for brownstone. It had become a fashionable building material in the cities along the eastern seaboard, eventually even reaching to the West Coast. The expanding market caused dramatic changes in the operation of the companies themselves. Steam power was harnessed to run pumps and derricks, and move and cut stone. Blasting was introduced to allow the less accessible stone to be quarried. Despite these improvements in technology, increased production still depended on a large labor force. This demand was met by the providential influx of Irish immigrants starting in the 1830s. With few exceptions, these men entered the labor force at the lowest level.

By the 1880s the average number of employees working at each of the three quarries had increased to about three hundred. While the Irish continued to form a large portion of this work force, by this time a high proportion of the workers were also Swedes. Swedish immigration appears to have begun in the 1860s. While the Swedes began to assume the more hazardous, non-skilled tasks, the Irish began to move into the skilled jobs such as foremen and stonecutters.

The quarry companies' management controlled not only the economic base, but also the civil authority. By 1840 Portland had, in a very real sense, become a "company town." Like most company towns, the financial success and interests of the managerial class determined the continuing economic prosperity and growth of the town.

While the quarry industry directly stimulated the growth of Portland's economic and industrial base, it also provided indirect stimulus. The vibrant

Left: The new photograph is Main Street in 1996. Courtesy Middlesex County Historical Society

Below: This postcard is taken looking toward Middletown— notice the old railroad bridge to the left. Courtesy of Bernadette S. Prue

187

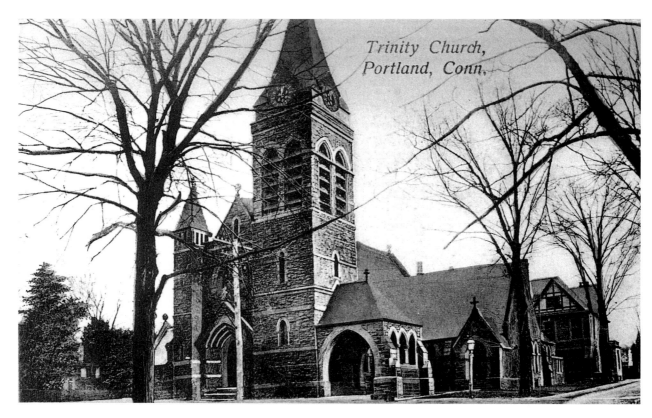

Trinity Church, Portland, Conn.

A postcard view shows the Trinity Church, constructed of Portland brownstone. Courtesy Middlesex County Historical Society

economy which was established in the town by the quarry operations began to attract other industries, such as the Pickering Governor Company (est. 1862), the Eastern Tinware Company (est. 1888), and the American Stamping Company (est. 1889). Nor was it long before an economic interrelationship began to develop between these manufacturing companies and the quarries through indirect reciprocal purchasing of stock shares by individual members of management from both industries.

The Architectural Legacy

By the 1850s the focus of the town's social and economic life had shifted to the lower Main Street area, in close proximity to the quarries. By the 1840s members of families who owned the principal interests in the quarries had begun to build large, fashionable homes along lower Main Street. Some of these residences, such as the Alfred Hall House, were constructed of

brownstone, an appropriate and highly tangible expression of the relationship of the quarrying industry and the development of this part of town. But while these fashionable structures were being erected, the older eighteenth- and early nineteenth-century houses remained, particularly those standing on the streets which ran west from Main toward the quarries. Many of these older residences were purchased by the quarry companies for housing for the expanding immigrant labor force, or run as boarding houses by private individuals.

Similarly, throughout the 1860s and 1870s, large fashionable houses were being built northward along lower Main Street. Middle-income neighborhoods began to develop on the lands abutting Main Street properties from the east, along the streets now known as Church Street, Waverly Avenue, Spring Street, and East Main Street.

By the beginning of the twentieth century, the demand for brownstone had begun to wane, principally because of the

Left: This lovely Queen Anne Style home, originally the residence of Judge Hame, is now Parish House for Trinity church. Courtesy Middlesex County Historical Society

Below: Fred Stancliff in his horse-drawn sleigh in front of one of the houses (where his grandfather lived). Courtesy Evelyn Pasternack

advent of poured concrete and curtain-wall construction techniques and the development of the skycraper. Curtain-wall construction allowed buildings to be built much higher than had ever been thought possible, an extremely important factor in cities where land was becoming increasingly scarce and more costly. The relatively low cost of concrete as compared to brownstone, and the decrease in construction time which curtain-wall techniques provided, also substantially reduced the cost per square foot for new construction.

Although Portland's quarries remained in operation until the 1930s, their output decreased rapidly after the turn of the twentieth century. As the town's economy was closely tied to quarrying, with the decline in demand for brownstone came a decline in the town's economic base. The loss of its major source of wealth was reflected in the subsequent decline of the town's two major secondary industries, shipbuilding and manufacturing. For Portland, the era of continual growth and increasing prosperity—the great brownstone era—was at an end.

Today, Portland is a small, quiet, suburban community maintaining close economic ties with both Middletown and Hartford. In this sense it closely resembles its neighboring communities, East Hampton and Cromwell. But while these similarities exist, Portland also retains a distinct character, derived from its heritage as the center of one of the country's most important and successful nineteenth-century mining industries, a character visibly reflected in the architecture of the town's central commercial district.

Far left: Fred and Arthur Stancliff built the octagon-shaped houses which still stand on Marlboro Street. Other views of the houses, including the way they look today. (old) Courtesy Evelyn Pasternack (new) Courtesy Bernadette S. Prue

Above: Elizabeth and Gilbert Stancliff, paternal grandparents of Arthur and Fred. Courtesy Evelyn Pasternack

Right: The Pascall family in front of their Main Street home, decorated for Portland's 75th anniversary celebration in 1916. Courtesy Daniel and Janalyn Davis

*Above: Building the Middletown-
Portland Highway Bridge.
Courtesy Bernard Prue*

*Middle & Below: Dedication
on April 15, 1896. The bridge
served for over 40 years before
being dismantled in 1939
after completion of the Arrigoni
Portland Bridge. Courtesy
Bernard Prue*

Portland's Town Clerk, Mr. Mitchell, hard at work in March 1906. Courtesy Nancy E. Schott

The Portland Middle School on Main Street was built of local brownstone. Courtesy Bernadette S. Prue

"Four Men in a Boat" on the
Connecticut River. Shown are:
John ———, John Bruce, Lee
Francis, Eugene Clark. Courtesy
Nancy E. Schott

Bibliography

The six town chapters are revised versions of the following (more extensive bibliographical references can be found in each):

Cunningham, Janice P. *The History and Architecture of Middlefield.* Middletown: Greater Middletown Preservation Trust, 1981.

Cunningham, Janice P. and Elizabeth A. Warner. *Portrait of a River Town: The History and Architecture of Haddam, Connecticut.* Middletown: Greater Middletown Preservation Trust, 1984.

Hall, Peter Dobkin. "The History and Architecture of Durham, Connecticut." Unpublished, 1983–1984.

Johnson, Judith E. and William H. Tabor. *The History and Architecture of Cromwell.* Middletown: Greater Middletown Preservation Trust, 1980.

Loether, J. Paul, Gail Linskey Porteus, and Doris Darling Sherrow. *The History and Architecture of Portland.* Middletown: Greater Middletown Preservation Trust, 1980.

Potter, Lucy G. and William A. Ritchie. *The History and Architecture of East Hampton.* Middletown: Greater Middletown Preservation Trust, 1980.

Cromwell

Academy Mirror, April 5, 1871. Cromwell Historical Society.

Ashley, Mrs. Marie. Correspondence with Thomas Stevens, Deep River, Connecticut, concerning steamboats "Experiment" and "Oliver Ellsworth." Cromwell.

Butler, Eva. Genealogical Material on the Savage Family. Cromwell, possession of Mr. and Mrs. Sewall Butler.

"Census of Old Buildings in Connecticut." WPA Writers Project MSS.Connecticut State Library, Hartford, Connecticut.

Cromwell Births, Marriage and Deaths, Vols. 1–7, 1850–1934.

Cromwell Chronicle January 1996. Chronicle Communications, 1996.

Cromwell Community Guide, 1995. Chronicle Communications, 1995.

"Cromwell, Connecticut Baptist Church Records 1802–1920" MSS. Connecticut State Library.

Cromwell Conservation Commission, Annual Reports, 1975, 1977.

Cromwell "Corporations and Manufacturers," Book 1.

Cromwell Land Records.

Cromwell Manufacturing Company, "Account Books 1851–1860" MSS. Cromwell Historical Society.

Cromwell Tax Abstracts.

Cromwell, Town of, "Cromwell Old Home Day, 1851–1961." A booklet, 1961.

Cromwell Town Charter, 1973.

Cromwell Town Meetings. Vols. 1 and 2. 1851–1917.

Cromwell's American Revolution Bicentennial Events 1974–1976. Bicentennial Commission, 1977.

Decker, Robert Owen with Margaret A. Harris, *Cromwell, Connecticut 1650–1990, The History of a River Port Town.* Cromwell Historical Society and Phoenix Publishing, West Kennebunk, Maine, 1991.

Dudley, M. S. "Town of Cromwell" in *History of Middlesex County, Connecticut,* edited by J. B. Beers. New York: J. B. Beers & Company, 1884.

Ely, Selden G. Collected Papers MSS. Connecticut State Library.

Federal Writers' Project of the Works Progress Administration for the State of Connecticut. *Connecticut: A Guide to Its Roads, Lore, and People.* Riverside Press, 1938.

Giardina, James. J. "Cromwell's Swedish Immigrants" MS. Wesleyan University, 1979.

Hale, Charles R., compiler, "Cromwell Cemetery Inscriptions." WPA Writers Project MS. Hartford, 1937.

Hartford Courant, "Ranney Family Reunion." July 27, 1994.

Loveless, Helene B. "A History of the Friendly Association and the Belden Library." Paper for the Cromwell Historical Society, 1975.

Maselli, Elizabeth A. compiler. "Business Letterhead Scrapbook" MS. Belden Libary, Cromwell, Connecticut.

_____ . Photograph Collection, 7 vols. MS.Belden Library.

_____ . "Cromwell Historical Collection" Vols. 1 and 2. Belden Library.

Middletown Land Records.

Middletown–Memorials.

Middletown Press. "The Centennial Edition of the Middletown Press, 1884–1984."

Middletown Probate Records.

Middletown Retailer's Licenses.

Middletown Tax Abstracts.

Middletown Tax Lists. Grand Levy. Vols. 1–5, 1770–1856.

Middletown Town Votes and Proprietors' Records. Vols. 1–3.

Nature Conservancy. *From the Land.* Middletown, Summer 1995.

Savage, Abijah. "Account Book 1792–1812" MS. Belden Library)

_____. "Company Book of Abijah Savage with Shipyard Accounts" MS. Connecticut State Library.

Savage, Seth. "Middletown and Berlin Turnpike, Treasures Account Book" MS. Connecticut State Library.

Stevens, Thomas A. *Stevens Collection.* Thomas Stevens Library, Essex, Connecticut.

Upper Houses, Bulletin of the Cromwell Historical Society, no. 1. June 1967.

Warner, John. "Account Book" ca. 1698–1750 MS. Connecticut State Library.

Durham

Beers, J. B. & Company. *Commemorative Biographical Record of Middlesex County Connecticut.* New York, 1901.

_____. *History of Greene County, New York.* New York, 1884.

_____. *History of Middlesex County, Connecticut.* New York, 1884.

Buel, Richard. *Dear Liberty: Connecticut's Mobilization for the Revolutionary War.* Middletown: Wesleyan University Press, 1980.

Bushman, Richard. *From Puritan to Yankee: Character and the Social Order in Connecticut, 1690–1765.* New York: W. W. Norton & Co., 1970.

Camp, Mary G. *Diary.* Connecticut State Library.

Chauncey Family. Papers. Yale University Library.

Durham History Committee. *Durham, Connecticut, 1866–1980 Century of Change.* Durham, 1980.

Durham, Town Clerk's Office. *Grand Lists, 1792–1916.*

_____. *Joint Stock Company Records, 1850–1914.*

_____. *Town Accounts, 1790–1830.*

____. *Vital Records, 1708–1947*.

Field, David Dudley. *Statistical Account of Middlesex County*. Middletown, 1819.

____. *Centennial History of Middlesex County*. Middletown, 1862.

Fitch, James M. *American Building: The Historical Forces That Shaped It*. New York: Schocken Books, 1973.

Foley, Mary Mix. *The American House*. New York: Harper & Row, 1980.

Fowler, William Chauncey. *Memorials of the Chaunceys*. Boston: H. W. Dutton and Sons, 1862.

____. *History of Durham*. Hartford, 1866.

Greven, Philip. *Four Generations: Population, Land, and Family in Colonial Andover, Massachusetts*. Ithaca, New York: Cornell University Press, 1970.

Hall, Charles S. *Hall Ancestry*. New York: G. P. Putnam's Sons, 1896.

Hall, Peter Dobkin. *The Organization of American Culture*. New York: New York University Press, 1982.

Hamlin, Talbot. *Greek Revival Architecture in America*. New York: Oxford University Press, 1944.

Handlin, David P. *The American Home: Architecture and Society, 1815–1915*. Boston: Little Brown, 1979.

Isham, Norman and Albert F. Brown. *Early Connecticut Houses*. Providence, R.I.: Preston & Rounde Co., 1900.

Jones, Edgar R. *Those Were the Good Old Days: A Happy Look at American Advertising, 1880–1930*. New York: Simon and Schuster, 1959.

Kelly, J. Frederick. *Early Domestic Architecture of Connecticut*. New Haven: Yale University Press, 1935.

Morgan, Edmund S. *The Puritan Family: Religion and Domestic Relations in Seventeenth–Century New England*. New York: Harper & Row, 1966.

Newton, Caroline Gaylord. *Miles Merwin, 1623–1697, and One Branch of His Descendants*. Durham, 1909.

____. *Rev. Roger Newton, Deceased 1683 and One Line of His Descendants*. Durham, 1912.

Report of the Case of Joshua Stow versus Sherman Converse. New Haven, 1822.

East Hampton

"Address of the Connecticut Society for the Encouragement of American Manufacturers." Middletown: T. Dunning, 1817.

Carrier, John A. Untitled recollections about Middle Haddam houses. Copy on file, Middle Haddam Library.

Chatham Probate Records.

Chatham/East Hampton Land Records.

Chatham/East Hampton Vital Records.

Child, Thomas. Account Book. Private collection, Margaret Dart.

Church Abstracts collected from Connecticut parishes. Connecticut State Library.

Connecticut, State of. "Report of the Secretary of State Relative to Certain Branches of Industry." MS. House of Representatives Document No. 26, May Session 1839.

Connecticut, State of, *Statistics of the Conditions and Products of Certain Branches of Industry in Connecticut for the Year Ending October 1, 1845*. Hartford: J. L. Boswell, 1846.

Dart, Margaret. "Old Houses of the Middle Haddam/Cobalt Area." Pictorial manuscript. Middle Haddam Library.

East Hampton Annual Reports.

East Hampton Joint Stock Records.

"East Hampton's Most Distinguished Citizens." *East Hampton News* August 3, 1950. East Hampton Library.

Federal Census of Agriculture, 1850, 1860.

Federal Census of Industry, 1850, 1860, 1870, 1880.

Federal Census of the United States, 1790–1860.

Flisher, Leonard H. "Steady Growth is Shown by Christ Church." *East Hampton News*, June 27, 1941.

"History of the Bethlehem Lutheran Church." East Hampton Library.

Hurd Family Papers. Mystic Seaport, Mystic, Connecticut.

Hurd Family Papers. Yale University Library.

Loomis, Israel Foote. "The Town of Chatham." *The Connecticut Magazine*. June/July, 1899.

Manwaring, Charles W. *A Digest of the Early Connecticut Probate Records*. Hartford: R. S. Peck & Co., 1904.

Middlesex Gazette.

Middletown Land Records.

Middletown Probate Records.

Middletown Sentinel and Witness. "100th Anniversary Second Congregational Church, Middle Haddam Connecticut." Pamphlet, 1955.

Minutes of Chatham Town Meetings.

Niles, Elisha. Diary. Typescript. Connecticut State Library.

The Penny Press.

Portland Land Records.

Price, Carl F. "Books and East Hampton: The Bibliography of a Connecticut Township." *East Hampton News*, reprint 1936. East Hampton Library.

____. "History of Methodism." Copy on file, Wesleyan University.

Public Records of the Colony of Connecticut. Hartford: Case, Lockwood & Brainard, 1881.

Records and Accounts of Selectmen, Chatham 1767–1798.

Records of Christ Church, Middle Haddam.

Records of the East Hampton Congregational Church and of the Ecclesiastical Society 1748–1930.

Records of the First Congregational Church at Middle Haddam.

Rockwell, Henry. Diary and Account Book MS. East Hampton Library.

Shepard, Abel. Account Book MS. Copy on file, Wesleyan University.

Smith, Joel West. Untitled history of East Hampton's industry. Copy on file, East Hampton Library.

Sperry, Erwin S. "The Charcoal Furnace of East Hampton, Connecticut Bellmakers: Its History, Uses and Advantages." *The Brass World and Plater's Guide.* January 1913.

Stevens, Thomas A. Maritime Collection. Thomas Stevens Library, Essex, Connecticut.

Weaver, Glen. "Industry in an Agrarian Economy, Early 18th Century Connecticut." *Connecticut Historical Society Bulletin* 19, 1954.

Haddam

Albion, Robert, William A. Baker, and Benjamin W. La Baree. *New England and the Sea.* Middletown: Wesleyan University Press, 1972.

"Barbour Abstracts of Church Records in Connecticut." Connecticut State Library Archives.

Bayles, Richard M. "Town of Haddam." In *History of Middlesex County, Connecticut*, edited by J. B. Beers. New York: J.B. Beers and Company, 1884.

Beers, J. H. *Commemorative Biographical Record of Middlesex County.* Chicago: J. H. Beers, 1903.

Brainerd, Eveline Warner. "Haddam since the Revolution." *Connecticut Magazine*, December 1899, pp. 591–604.

____ . "The Plantation of Thirty Mile Island." *Connecticut Magazine*, November 1899, pp. 543–552.

Brainerd, Lucy Abigail. *The Genealogy of the Brainerd–Brainard Family in America 1649–1908.* Hartford: Hartford Press, 1908.

Brainerd, Ezra. Magistrate Records and Papers. Undated, privately owned manuscript; copy on file at Greater Middletown Preservation Trust.

Brigham, Willard Tyler. *Tyler Genealogy: Descendants of Job Tyler*, vol. 2. Plainfield, New Jersey and Tylerville, Connecticut: Cornelius B. Tyler and Rollin U .Tyler, 1912.

Brooks, Lillian Kruger. *Life Flows Along Like a River: A History of Haddam Neck.* Haddam Genealogical Group, 1972.

Buel, Richard, Jr. *Dear Liberty: Connecticut's Mobilization for the Revolutionary War.* Middletown: Wesleyan University Press, 1980.

Bushman, Richard L. *From Puritan to Yankee: Character and Social Order in Connecticut, 1690–1765.* Cambridge, Massachusetts: Harvard University Press, 1967.

Clarke, Levi Hubbard. "Haddam in 1808." Edited by Thompson R. Harlow in *Connecticut Historical Society Magazine.* Hartford: The Acorn Club of Connecticut, 1949, pp. 3–10.

Connecticut House Journal. Vol. 14. Connecticut General Assembly: Hartford, 1859.

Connecticut Senate Journal. Vol. 13. Connecticut General Assembly: Hartford, 1859.

Cunningham, Janice P. "From Fathers to Sons: The Emergence of the Modern Family in Rural Connecticut, 1700–1850." May 1979, M.A. Thesis, Wesleyan University, 1979.

Curtice, Reverend Saul O. *Centennial of the West Haddam Methodist Episcopal Church.* New Haven: J. T. Hathaway, 1897.

Daniels, Bruce C. *The Connecticut Town: Growth and Development, 1635–1790.* Middletown: Wesleyan University Press, 1979.

Destler, Chester M. *Connecticut: The Provision State.* Chester, Connecticut: Pequot Press, 1973.

Doane, Doris. *A Book of Cape Cod Houses.* Greenwich, Connecticut: Chatham Press, 1970.

Donlan, H. G. "The Middletown Tribune Souvenir Edition: An Illustrated and Descriptive Exposition of Middletown, Portland, Cromwell, East Berlin, and Higganum." Middletown, Connecticut: E. F. Bigelow, 1896.

Dwight, Timothy. *Travels in New England and New York.* Edited by Barbara Miller Solomon. 4 vols. Cambridge,Massachusetts Belknap Press, 1969.

Farber, Bernard. *Guardians of Virtue: Salem Families in 1800.* New York: Basic Books, 1972.

Federal Census of the United States. Connecticut, New York, 1790, 1800.

Federal Census of the United States. Connecticut, 1850, 1860.

Field, David Dudley. *A History of the Towns of Haddam and East Haddam.* Middletown, Connecticut: Loomis and Richards, 1814.

____. *A Statistical Account of the County of Middlesex.* Middletown, Connecticut: Clark and Lyman, 1819.

____. *The Genealogy of the Brainerd Family in the United States.* New York: John F. Trowbridge Printer, 1857.

Garvan, Anthony N. B. *Architecture and Town Planning in Colonial Connecticut.* New Haven: Yale University Press, 1951.

Gross, Robert A. *The Minutemen and their World.* New York: Hill and Wang, American Century Series, 1976.

Haddam Congregational Church Ecclesiastical Records. Connecticut State Library.

Haddam Land Records.

Haddam Probate Records.

Haddam Town Records.

"Haddam U.S.A., Official Program–Town of Haddam, 1662–1962." Haddam, Connecticut: Haddam Tercentenary Inc., 1962.

Haddam Vital Records.

Hall, Peter Dobkin. "Marital Selection and Business in Massachusetts Merchant Families, 1700–1900." In *The American Family in Social–Historical Perspective.* 2nd edition. Edited by Michael Gordon. New York: St. Martin's Press, 1978.

____. "Middletown: Streets, Commerce, and People, 1650–1981." *Wesleyan University Sesquicentennial Papers,* No. 8, 1981.

Henretta, James A. *The Evolution of American Society, 1700–1815: An Interdisciplinary Analysis.* Lexington, Massachusetts and Toronto: D. C. Heath and Co., 1973.

____. "Families and Farms: *Mentalité* in Pre–Industrial America." *William and Mary Quarterly* third series, no. 33 (January 1978).

Knowles, The Reverend William C. *By Gone Days of Ponset-Haddam.* New York: Printed by the author, 1914.

Lewis, Everett E. *Historical Sketch: First Congregational Church in Haddam, Connecticut.* Middletown: Pelton and King, 1879.

Manual of the Congregational Church, Higganum, Conn. Middletown, Connecticut: Pelton and King, 1883.

Manwaring, Charles W. *A Digest of the Early Connecticut Probate Records.* Hartford: R. S. Peck and Co., 1904.

Middlebrook, Louis F. *Maritime Connecticut During the Revolution.* 2 vols. Salem, Massachusetts: The Essex Insitute, 1925.

Middletown Probate Records.

Middlesex County Court Records 1785–1805.

Monahan, Thomas P. *The Pattern of Age at Marriage in the United States.* Vol. 1. Philadelphia: Stephenson Brothers, 1951.

Phipps, Frances and Paul Weld. *The Thankful Arnold House, Haddam, Connecticut.* n.p., n.d.

Public Records of the Colony of Connecticut. Hartford: Case, Lockwood and Brainerd, 1881.

Purcell, Richard J. *Connecticut in Transition, 1775–1818.* Middletown: Wesleyan University Press, 1963.

Registers of Vessels, Middletown Customs District. 10 vols. From the original manuscripts in the National Archives, Washington, D. C. Compiled by Lila W. Davis for Thomas A. Stevens. Repository for records: Thomas A. Stevens Library, Connecticut River Foundation at Steamboat Dock, Inc., Essex, Connecticut.

Scranton, A. *Report of the Joint Standing Committee on New Towns and Probate Districts.* Connecticut General Assembly. "Upon the Petition of Elliot Brainerd and others, for the incorporation of a New Town from Haddam, to be called Higganum." May Session, 1859.

Selden, Henry. "Haddam Neck." In *History of Middlesex County, Connecticut,* edited by J. B. Beers. New York: J.B. Beers and Company, 1884.

Shailer, Ursula "Ursula's Notebook." Manuscript in Shailer Papers. Connecticut State Library Archives.

Shaler, Harrison. "The Thomas Shaylor Family–Descendants of Thomas Shailer of Haddam." *Connecticut Nutmegger* vol. 12, no. 4 (March 1890).

Stevens, Thomas A. "New York Registered Ships from Haddam" in "Ship Registers of New York, New York 1801–1861." Typescript, 1938. Transcribed from the originals. Thomas A. Stevens Library, Essex, Connecticut.

Two–Hundredth Anniversary of the First Congregational Church of Haddam, Connecticut, 1700–1900. Haddam: The DeVinne Press, 1902.

Tyler, Rollin U. "The Early Settlers and Their Homes." *In Two–Hundredth Anniversary of the First Congregational Church of Haddam, Connecticut, 1700–1900.* Haddam: The DeVinne Press, 1902.

Vinovskis, Maris A. "Angel's Heads and Weeping Willows: Death in Early America." In *The American Family in Social–Historical Perspective*. 2nd edition. Edited by Michael Gordon. New York: St. Martin's Press, 1978.

The Wyllys Papers Correspondence and Documents Chiefly of Descendants of Gov. George Wyllys of Connecticut 1590–1796. Collections of the Connecticut Historical Society, vol. 21. Hartford, 1924.

Middlefield

Atkins, Thomas. *History of Middlfield and Long Hill*. Hartford: Case, Lockwood & Brainard Co., 1883.

"Barbour Abstracts of Church Records in Connecticut." Connecticut State Library Archives.

"Barbour Abstracts of Town Vital Records." Connecticut State Library Archives.

Bartlett, J. Gardner. *Robert Coe, Puritan: His Ancestors and Descendants, 1340–1900, with notices of other Coe Families*. Boston, Mass.: self published, 1911.

Beers, J. B. *History of Middlesex County, Connecticut*. New York: J. B. Beers & Company, 1884.

Blejwas, Stanislaus. "Researching Ethnic History in Connecticut: The Polish Question." *Connecticut History* 22 (January 1981): 31–41.

Brown, Richard D. *Modernization: The Transformation of American Life, 1600–1865*. New York: Hill and Wang, 1976.

Bushman, Richard. *From Puritan to Yankee: Character and Social Order in Connecticut, 1690–1765*. New York: W.W. Norton and Co., 1970.

Coe, Levi Elmore. *Coe–Ward Memorial and Immigrant Ancestors*. Meriden, Conn.: Press of Converse Publishing Co., 1897.

Coleman, Lyman, D. D. *Genealogy of the Lyman Family in Great Britain and America*. Albany, N.Y.: J. Munsell, 1872.

Curtis Genealogy of Stratford, Connecticut. Ann Arbor, Michigan: Edward Bros., 1903, 1953.

Cunningham, Janice P. "From Fathers to Sons: The Emergence of the Modern Family in Rural Connecticut, 1700–1850." May 1979, M.A. thesis, Wesleyan University, 1979.

Daniels, Bruce C. "Money Value Definitions of Economic Classes in Connecticut, 1700–1776." *Histoire Sociale—Social History* (November 1974): 348.

———. T*he Connecticut Town*. Middletown: Wesleyan University Press, 1979.

Deetz, James. *In Small Things Forgotten: The Archaeology of Early American Life*. New York: Doubleday, Anchor Books, 1977.

Demos, John. *A Little Commonwealth: Family Life in Plymouth Colony*. New York: Oxford University Press Inc., 1970.

Dyson, Stephanie. Gravestone Inscriptions and Genealogy—Old North Burying Ground. Middlefield, Connecticut. MS. 1980.

Farber, Bernard. *Guardians of Virtue*. New York: Basic Books, 1972.

Field, David D. *A Statistical Study of the County of Middlesex*. Middletown: Clark and Lyman, 1819.

Federal Census of the United States, 1840–1880.

Garvan, Anthony N.B. *Architecture and Town Planning in Colonial Connecticut*. New Haven: Yale University Press, 1951.

Greven, Philip J., Jr. *Four Generations: Population, Land and Family in Colonial Andover, Massachusetts*. Ithaca and London: Cornell University Press, 1970.

Lockridge, Kenneth A. *A New England Town: The First Hundred Years*. New York: W.W. Norton & Company Inc., 1970.

Lyman Centennial Journal 1879–1978. Middlefield: Lyman Publications, 1978 .

Lyman, David II. Account Books 1849–1871 MSS. Collection of the Lyman Family.

Manwaring, Charles W. *A Digest of the Early Connecticut Probate Records*. Hartford: R.S. Peck & Co., 1904.

Middlefield Land Records.

Middletown Land Records.

Middletown Probate Records.

Middletown Tax Records, "A list of all Inhabitants of the Town of Middletown in the year MDCCXCVI Except those exempted by Law". 1796–1850.

Middletown Votes and Proprietors Records.

Morgan, Edmund S. The Puritan Family: Religion and Domestic Life in Seventeenth– Century New England. New York: Harper and Row, 1966.

Parsons, Henry. Descendants of Cornet Joseph Parsons: Springfield 1636—North Hampton 1655. Vol. 1. New York: Frank Allaben Genealogical Co. n.d.; vol. 2. New Haven, Conn.; Tuttle, Morehouse and Taylor Co., n.d.

Gutman, Herbert G. *Work Culture and Society in Industrializing America*. New York: Vintage Books, 1977.

Hall, Peter Dobkin. "Marital Selection and Business in Massachusetts Merchant Families, 1700–1900." In *The American Family in Social–Historical Perspectives*, 2nd ed. Edited by Michael Gordon. New York: St. Martin's Press, 1978.

Henretta, James A. *The Evolution of American Society 1700–1815: An Interdisciplinary Analysis.* Lexington, Mass. and Toronto: D. C. Heath and Co., 1973.

Joshua Stow vs. Sherman Converse for a Libel: Containing a History of Two Trials Before the Superior Court. New Haven: S. Converse, 1822.

Keyssar, Alexander. "Widowhood in Eighteenth Century Massachusetts." In *Perspectives in American History* 8 (1974): 83–119.

Lerner, Daniel. *The Passing of Traditional Society.* New York: The Free Press, 1958.

Miller Family Papers. Misc. MSS. Private Collection of Paul Francis.

Miller, Phineas. Correspondence MSS. Miller Family Papers, Connecticut State Library Archives.

Purcell, Richard J. *Connecticut in Transition, 1775–1818.* Middletown: Wesleyan University Press, 1963.

Public Records of the Colony of Connecticut. Hartford: Case, Lockwood and Brainard, 1881.

Records of the Congregational Church of Middlefield. Connecticut State Library.

Schumacher, Max George. *The Northern Farmer and His Markets During the Late Colonial Period.* New York: Arno Press, 1975.

Slotkin, Richard E. *Regeneration through Violence.* Middletown: Wesleyan University Press, 1973.

Smith, Daniel Scott. "Parental Power and Marriage Patterns: An Analysis of Historical Trends in Hingham, Massachusetts." In *The American Family in Social–Historical Perspective*, 2nd ed. pp. 88, 89. Edited by Michael Gordon. New York: St. Martin's Press, 1978.

"Souvenir Program: 50th Anniversary of the Tadeusz Kosciuszko Society." Rockfall,Connecticut: 1980.

Stow, Joshua. Diaries 1783–1788 MSS. Middlesex County Historical Society Archives.

Wetmore, James Carnahan. *The Wetmore Family in America: Its Collateral Branches with Genealogical, Biographical and Historical Notes.* Albany: Munsell and Rowland, 1861.

Portland

Alsop, Jesse. Letters to Pegleg Williams MS. Private Collection.

Chatham Land Records.

Chatham Probate Records.

Chatham Tax Records.

Chatham Vital Records.

Church Abstracts. Collected from Connecticut Parishes, on file, Connecticut State Library.

Connecticut Indian Archives. Connecticut State Library.

Connecticut, State of. "Report of the Secretary of State Relative to Certain Branches of Industry." MS. House of Representatives Document No. 29, May Session 1839.

Federal Census of Industry, 1850, 1860, 1870, 1880.

Federal Census of the United States, 1790–1860.

Flood, Mary. "History of Buck Library" MS. Buck Library.

Gildersleeve, Sylvester. Memoirs MS. Connecticut State Library.

Manwaring, Charles W. *A Digest of the Early Connecticut Probate Records.* Hartford: R.S. Peck & Company, 1904.

Middletown Land Records.

Middletown Probate Records.

Middletown Town Votes and Proprietors Records. Vols. 1 and 2.

Minutes of Chatham Town Meetings.

Portland Burial Records.

Portland Records of Joint Stock Companies.

Portland Land Records.

Portland Probate Records.

Portland Tax Records 1841–1930. Grand Levy.

Portland Vital Records.

Public Records of the Colony of Connecticut. Hartford: Case, Lockwood & Brainard, 1881.

Records and Accounts of Selectmen, Chatham 1767–1798.

Records of the First Congregational Church of Portland, Connecticut. Connecticut State Library.

Shaler and Hall Quarry. Accounts 1840–1860 MS. Connecticut Historical Society.

Shepard, Abel. Account Book MS. Copy on file, Wesleyan University.

Stevens, Thomas A. *Stevens Collection.* Thomas A. Stevens Library, Essex, Conn.

Wielgorecki, Claudia. "Portland, Connecticut in the Brownstone Era" MS. Copy on file, Greater Middletown Preservation Trust.

White, Ebenezer. Journal MS. Connecticut Historical Society.

Index

•*Italicized page numbers refer to captions*

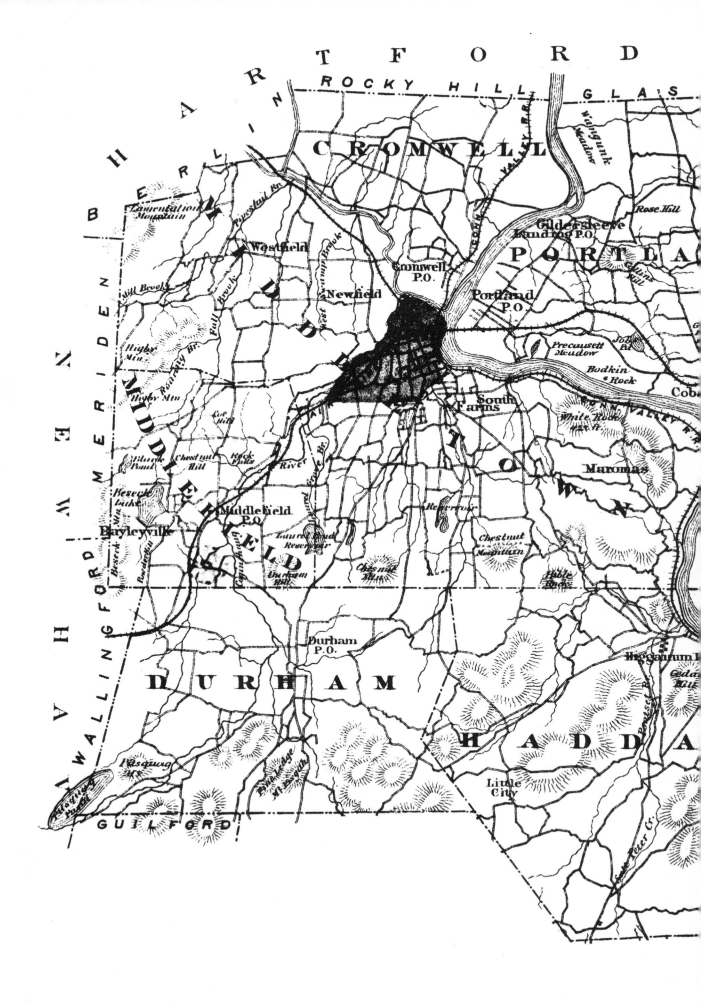